BOOKS BY THE SAME AUTHOR

The Cape Breton Book of the Dead (1975)

Heaven (1978)

War in an Empty House (1982)

Hammerstroke (1986)

Wolf-Ladder (1991)

Stations of the Left Hand (1994)

Parish of the Physic Moon (1998)

All Our Wonder Unavenged (2007)

Bite Down Little Whisper (2013)

Fetishes of the Floating World (2021)

DON DOMANSKI

SELECTED POEMS

1975–2021

XYLEM BOOKS 2022

RECENT XYLEM TITLES

XY07 Living In The World As If It Were Home (2019)

XY08 Moosewood Sandhills (2019)

XY09 An Almost-Gone Radiance (2020)

XY10 And Then Gone (2020)

XY11 A Flint Incentive (2020)

XY12 Limnology (2020)

XY13 Harmonia Mundi (2022)

XY14 Selected Poems, 1975–2021 (2022)

Don Domanski, *Selected Poems*, 1975–2021

First published in 2021 by Corbel Stone Press

With thanks to Brick Books for permission to reprint poems from
All Our Wonder Unavenged and *Bite Down Little Whisper*

ISBN: 978-1-9163935-8-5

Cover image:

Falcon statue serving as a sarcophagus for a sacred animal

Egypt, 664–30 B.C.

Xylem Books is an imprint of Corbel Stone Press

CONTENTS

From *War in an Empty House* (1982)

From *Stations of the Left Hand* (1994)

From *Parish of the Physic Moon* (1998)

From *All Our Wonder Unavenged* (2007)

From *Bite Down Little Whisper* (2013)

Don Domanski repeatedly took himself to magical, liminal places in his poetry, "the edge of a forest/that is capable of anything" ("Edge"). He went to such places as an intermediary, a metaphysical adventurer, and he brought us with him, enticing us out of our cramped Cartesian enclaves where everything is too bright and over-known. And thus he placed us in touch with energy and mystery, and was a refugium and healer since he acknowledged, befriended and moved in a multiplicity of worlds.

Domanski's worlds aren't the product of capricious invention, but the recovered essential elements of the *real* one, the "vast earth" familiar to contemplative philosophers like Ibn 'Arabi and the people who left their art on the walls of Chauvet cave over 30,000 years ago. Because he lived as an artist in this varied place, he was under-celebrated in a literary climate favouring a one-ply realism. And because of his recognition of a multi-layered reality, chthonic and metaphysical together, he was a rare poet capable of changing lives. No one else wrote like him. He has left us with so much in his books, and all of it strikes me as not just poetically thrilling but psychagogically solid; if he shows us stairs to ascend or descend, we know we can trust our weight to them.

A great burnisher of the ordinary, Don Domanski made us look at the details of our days with a scintillating freshness. In line after line, the supra-real clusters around unattended ordinary objects and processes. He spies the remarkable from his own middle-of-the-night perspective:

> above me moths chaperone the musculature
> of stars and the Delphic shudder of a cloud
> prophesying a bright green world

("Ursa Immaculate")

Reading passages like this, we, too, bump up against a sentience, a *conatus*, at play in things, a force that is both purposeful and intimate. We are dislodged from a reductive, object-indifferent seeing and liberated into a broader, more interesting, ontological citizenship. It takes courage to be this different—*atopos*, unusual, out of place, Plato would say—both as a writer and one who looks, and from the very beginning of his career, in *The Cape Breton Book of the Dead* (1975) and *Heaven* (1978), his work was bold, reaching farther.

*

I first met Don in the mid 1990s when he came to Saskatoon to read at two poetry series I then ran, one in the city and the other at

St. Peter's College a hundred kilometres to the east. After picking
him up at the airport late on a freezing Sunday night, I took him to
an otherwise unoccupied Chinese restaurant downtown and we
plunged into a conversation that ate the hours. We discovered that
we shared class roots, he growing up in tough areas of Sydney, Cape
Breton, I in northwest Regina. Somehow we'd both found a way to
poetry through, in my case, gangs, recreational crime and horrific
fights.

I don't know where in his past he may have found the exquisite
gentleness with which he treated the small and theurgic things he
noted, his teasing and courteous way with divinity-infused rain,
blue lice, fox tracks. His poetic treatment of these presences made
them pop out of the flat face of normal ontology, the greyness of
bland regard, and become mythic and mighty, central to the parlia-
ment of all that is; they holds worlds; they *are* worlds.

*

Tim Robinson, in his *Listening to the Wind: The Connemara Trilogy:
Part One*, observes how anglicized Irish place names dry out and
degrade Irish places, leaving them open to exploitation "for lack
of a comprehensible name to pinpoint their natures." Domanski
managed to make out unacknowledged powers and to retrieve
his degraded things through close observation, lavish imagistic
invention and music, and so revivified a more ample world capable
of sustaining us, making the self both more effacing and larger. The
roll of his language, the lushness of image coming after image, the
undulating musicality of his thought sings through the attentive
reader. His music is at times even more piercing than his jolting
imagery.

In my mind, Domanski was after that presence in objects and events, an *innerness*, that, post-Kant, was said to be unreachable, perhaps not even there. As he moved from cranny to cranny in the ground, in the air, deep in the grass, in the ghost-world of rivers, to the wolf's "swampy breath" that "presses against the door" ("Wolf-Ladder"), places unexplored in this culture, he followed animals and insects, their tracks, advice or charisma, without hesitation. He followed rain to "the held pulse of the soil", "all the spiders this side of Elysium" ("A Thin Place"), he followed bear and coyotes. These, in turn, become singular, reliable guides to further rambles into the inscapes of earth, but how to locate, then approach them? With the stretching permission imagination brings to knowing, the daredevilry of the presumptive leap. Half way through the arc, the arc of metaphor or narrative audacity, of Domanski's ontological leaps, you realize that though you have nothing beneath you at the moment, your gamble with these spirits will pay off, indeed that your travel to these otherwise inaccessible corners is the only course open for you. You are brought to "the black river under the earth" ("A Thin Place"), face to face with numinal flashes of "the spirit of other things" ("Osprey and Salmon").

Credo ut intelligam, wrote Anselm of Canterbury, *I believe so that I may know.* Faith makes for large noesis. All true. But so does imagination, the knotting of wildly unlike things—unlike yet still calling out to one another—in image and narrative unfolding, the setting aside, or ignoring, of the propriety of old categories, following some interior hunch concerning the vastness and complexity of creation. Reading the connections Domanski made, one dwells in a feral, more merciful, bigger-girthed landscape because someone has dreamt it, named it, peered into its individualities and that dream has entered the reader.

The small hours were Don's anchorage and his time of resolution, of *quies*, that rest and "negation of wounds," where a silence may appear "that passes/over us unseen like a dark forest/scarcely a centimetre or so above our heads" ("A Thin Place"). He conjured this resolved world repeatedly in his work, and this practice made that world real, inhabitable, a precarious state that one could dwell in by often going there, following that particular spiritual exercise. What breathtakingly ingenious generosity there was in this labour, extending the gift to all of us, the thing or power we hope to see "bending/the meadow grasses ever so slightly," its yearned-for gaze directed at us.

*

He liked to add quotations to some of his correspondence; one sent to me on October 30, 2011 ended with a paragraph from the twentieth century neo-Thomist Jacques Maritain.

> Metaphysics enjoys its possession only in the retreats of the eternal regions, while poetry finds its own at every crossroad in the wanderings of the contingent and singular. Metaphysics give chase to essences and definitions, poetry to any flash of existence glittering by the way, and any reflection of an invisible order.

Don's reach for the unlike was a form of knowing, "a pre-verbal reality, a calling forth from a core within our being," as he puts it in his Ralph Gustafson lecture "Poetry and the Sacred." He was all for the "invisible order" Maritain mentions, and because his allegiance to that occult republic was utterly serious, he knew the wildness of his thought and creating placed him in some peril, the danger known by the insurrectionist. With the American poet Donald Hall, he saw poetry as a "revolutionary act" in a culture committed to burying the sacred.

If this is true and poetry is numinous sedition, what is the state that emerges if Domanski's epistemological insurrection, poetry's insurrection, is successful? You could say that new place looks like the works of Don Domanski. It is a world in which intuition is valued highly, the gnosis that allows you to "fly over language," above "the ruins of custom and interpretation, mighty edifices meant to last millennia" ("Flying Over Language"). In this new place of imagination, we are near the Kingdom of Heaven, rescued from the asphyxiation of individualism and the tiny room of the present insistent preoccupation, in league with the dead—his dead including Eckhart, Rumi, Hildegard of Bingen, Lao-Tzu—and "a deer's porcelain footprints" and "a vapour/of rabbits in the hills" ("Nocturne"). Here, in this broader community, our heart's need for wonder, a hunger Domanski knew well, is appeased.

*

Don Domanski was a generous friend to many writers, generous in reading work and commenting on it, generous about setting us on our feet when we toppled, and also generous in his gifts. Even there, in friendship, he had a love for the far-away and resonant—like the natural cast of rain drops from the Lower Carboniferous from 350 million years ago that he gave me some time in the late 1990s. I, in contrast, was much more fumbling in my gift-giving, carrying back from a trip to western China a ring I'd purchased in a bazaar a short walk from Ta 'er Si, Kumbum Monastery, on the Tibetan plateau,

in old Amdo Province. I had taken the ring to be silver and of deep
Buddhist significance only to be told a few days after I'd presented
him with it by a gleeful Domanski that the ring was not silver at all
and bore the image of the Ka 'ba. He was as gentle with hopeless
gift-givers as he was with his small creatures.

*

Last summer, a few months before his death, he sent me a poem
from his weem of Nova Scotia's night:

> tonight the totality of all beings weighs
> less than a feather
> less than the movement of eyeshine
>   radiant in the thicket
> less than the weight of tomorrow
> balanced on a single blade of grass
>
> I love nights like this   hours quiet
> and driftless   the biosignatures
> of invisibilia filling the air   close
> as flesh to vein   as vein to earth
> close as the cuddle death of a queen
> deep in her hive.

*

> this night appears in the green world
> almost existing   almost not existing
> like subatomic particles

like the prehistory of a sigh
like the grace of sentience   spellwork
of consciousness throughout the foliage
it emerges from somewhere between
the intimacy of insects
        and the forgettance of men.

                        ("Small Hours")

I do not let myself think that I will never read again poetry fresh off
Domanski's nocturnal desk. I can't bring myself to take this fact in.

                        Tim Lilburn
                        Saanich, 2021

Notes

The tile of this essay is a line from "Sunrise at Sea Level".

The quotation from Tim Robinson's *Listening to the Wind: The Connemara Trilogy: Part One* appears in a review of that book in *The New York Review of Books*, Dec. 3, 2020.

The Jacques Maritain paragraph comes from his *Creative Intuition in Art and Poetry*, 1953.

The lecture "Poetry and the Sacred" was delivered at Vancouver Island University (then Malaspina College) in 2005.

"Flying Over Language" appears as an afterword in *Earthly Pages, The Poetry of Don Domanski*, 2007.

"Small Hours" is published in *Works for Now: an espresso anthology*, 2020.

Over the past several years Don Domanski was a friend and mentor, and latterly he had desired for us to publish a *New and Selected* anthology, beginning with his first collection, *The Cape Breton Book of the Dead*, and culminating in a new sequence of poems. Sadly, his untimely death on September 7th, 2020, has silenced the promise of new work, but this *Selected Poems* is, at least, a partial fulfilment of that living wish, and is a vital document of his lasting legacy.

The poems gathered here are 108 in number, a sacred figure in Vedic and Buddhist cultures, representing the wholeness of existence, and an allusion to Don's lifelong interest in Eastern philosophies. He had entrusted to us the selection of poems to be anthologised, and we have ultimately been guided by our own pre-dilections—our love of his bestiary of the strange and the familiar; the cats, dogs, ants, water fleas, sparrows, salamanders and fiery searchers. For us, his returning again and again to these *others* is not merely an artistic device or leitmotif, but a reflection of his deepfelt awe for the living world, his endless fascination and gratitude:

> The greatest mystery, held in every grain of cosmic dust, in every blade of grass, is existence itself. This is the first and last wonder, beyond words to describe; only the wordless poem can accomplish this.
>
> ("Poetry and the Sacred")

Notwithstanding his assertion that such wonder is beyond language to communicate, the poetry of Don Domanski, we would argue, brings us tantalisingly close, and reminds us that the sacred is to be found in the quotidian, "because any god is simply givenness/ brought to our attention" ("Stations of the Left Hand").

*

In this new XYLEM BOOKS edition of the *Selected Poems* we have retained the *Uncollected* section, which features the poems first published by Corbel Stone Press, beginning with the 2014 pamphlet "Field Notes", and followed by those featured in the journal *Reliquiae*: "Bestiary of the Raindrop", "Birthday", "A Thin Place", "Nocturne" and "The Goneness of Lost Things". These poems have been subsequently republished in the posthumous collection, *Fetishes of the Floating World*. As before, the *Uncollected* section ends with "A Prayer of Thanks", written for the Summer Solstice of 2017, and the book closes with his seminal essay, "Poetry and the Sacred".

Autumn Richardson & Richard Skelton,
Scottish Borders, 2022

Don Domanski

1950–2020

For Mary

FROM

THE CAPE BRETON BOOK
OF THE DEAD

1975

GERANIUMS

massive tempers
shaking their roots and displacing a tom's howl
with their own sudden cry
from the windowsill

all day trembling for light and water
yet at times rejoicing in tribal amazement
at their particular luck with living

when night comes I lie down with them
not as lover but to awake rooted
to become a wildman in a geranium pot
a recluse ten years gone.

CAT

for Lü

1

your body and mind
are death sentences
in unison.

2

this morning on my bed
you've left me
your final statement on everything

its face dried red
its stomach completely gone.

3

you are the Buddha
blood stained
with a perfect conscience.

NECROPOLIS

the rat's stomach is opened to the stars
a nebula placed in its bowel

rat face
and rat hide wait
in the city that grows like a rat's dream might
if rat knew algebra and alphabet

and had control of ballpoint
and pad

waits on the doorstep
for a rat's burial
in trash can or fire.

no one in that dark house
is now thinking about four rat paws
hardening on painted wood

no one expects to step on a necropolis
in the morning.

TODAY ALL KILLING

today all killing happens in this body
beneath this flesh:

the man hunted down in his room
the shark swimming into its meat
the moth boiling in the spider's brain
the sparrow flying a worm to the roof

tired and cold
each death stops here to rest
to lay down its cracked head and dream.

EDGE

I've come to the edge of a forest
that is capable of anything

wolves will not enter
but become ground beetles
and leave

this place is a turning point

the forest has lips and eyes
and rivers

they all stop and wait

beneath me
worms turn the earth
on its axis.

TO A BOY LOST IN THE FOREST AND BELIEVED DEAD
(HIS BODY NEVER HAVING BEEN FOUND)

your body is no longer your own
the catbird has it
and the fox
each holds an end
and moves swiftly away from the other

your body doesn't snap
it stretches
it yawns flesh from ground
to sky

it moves through the countryside
a thin pink world
which no one sees.

THE WOLF'S CITY

is himself.

where all buildings have smells
and noses to smell back

where all the crowds rush about
to buy one thing
then devour it immediately

where the musk of elk and caribou
drifts down every night covering the roofs of cars
and high-rises.

is a place where no one
is
but him

where all entrances
are erased each night
by the rubbing of a snout.

MADONNA

springtails found her
in the morning

with a belly full of water
and a lunar face
among the frogbit.

there was no prophecy.

she merely came
with the downpour
to bless the backswimmers
and the water shrew

and although for days after
did not labour
to bring forth child-god
or word
was loved

by the busy populace

the single water flea
that clung faithfully to her lips
her head knocking against the shore.

ANGELS

balanced like gulls
above the relapse of sea and rock
their heads slowly turn
a complete twist toward land

they carry burning swords and pen-names
like Michael and Israfel
but know themselves as larvae
twirling in a man's ear
or a rat gnawing away at a wall

dead Heaven's moil
they now drift spore-like toward anyone's mind
their silence thumping loudly
on the boulders drowning the water's edge

the Big Dipper rising
to bare its incisors over the sea.

NIGHTWALK

this night splayed from my head
is gossamer and cool

a dog-genius walks with me
points out the optical owls
fetches the stick flung at Taurus

around us without abandon
the combines of tree and rock
stand dazed in their own enlightenment

never witness our path
or hear
the dog call everything
by its proper name.

FROM

HEAVEN

1978

SUMMER-PIECE

whose heart or bowel was looted
for this cool arena of trees?
for this footage of bracken
ajar at my feet?

who paid for that sparrow's
nervous direction through the thicket?
for his song roofing
these goldenrods and lupines?

there is someone's vigour
wasting away under
all this blood and greenery

there is someone's familiar face
sagging over every bloom
permeating each athletic gesture
of the land

someone's torso that I knew so well
was ousted for this slew of flies
in the afternoon air

for this pond's peculiar look.

HEAVEN

something couples (dearheart) with the motes
with the mulish roots
holds the bleb of newts
holds the fox's starved look

something moves with the spume
of the sea's edge walking dry land

lies with the indigestible fug
under stones
under the green of the hillock
pushing toward light

it has always been there
in the tree's head
in the bits of grass

a flame floating with the hare
on darkness

a revelation sighing with the bag
of snakes

with the talking hedge
lit with flies.

CAMPING OUT

for hours I sat kennelled
beneath the sleeping tarp

listening to a spasm of ferns
push to the pond's edge

to a tongue wag
in the thick neb of the land

to the clarity of stones
mouth the heart.

all night a half moon
and a wind goading
the stain of my small fire

here is the black rent
at the end of memory
here is the starlit anonymity

face down in the world.

MADE IN HEAVEN

this dead shrew is a vista

is a wedge opening
these marshlands to a premonition
to a gathering of dread in the blood

for hours I have heard the crows
busy themselves with mortality
have felt the flies
pin the hot air against my face

all morning the two mile outlook
of stench and bog
has risen to a deafening intone

to a full stratum of immovable energy
that pushes my eyes back

to a single heartbeat
to a single head

emptied of its operations.

OWL SONG

Lord of this wood
King flying through his bitchery
(feathered for narcissism)
loaded with immeasurable purpose
answering no one
light around his rank head
not saintlight but a rage of blue
made from endless responsibility

carrying off the indifferent dead
one by one.

SUNRISE AT SEA LEVEL

out of the eye's corner
comes the red visor of the orchis
the torturous reds of war

out from behind the injured white
steps the magenta of thorns
and knives

the eye-shaped sun
approaching the tide

I am always here
a bystander applauding
the inflammation of the waves
the constant flaring of water

all winter and all summer
I have come to this seawall
to numerous fires
to the effigy-burning lights of the sea
hoping for something to appear

something gigantic

something to fill a vacancy
that does not carry

the sweet poor scent
of the flesh

a ghost would do
or a jackal-headed god
in a boat

or at night the green polar lights
could appear like a siren
like bird-legged Molpe
seated on her rock

throwing men causally into the sea.

SPIDER SONG

for Eleanor Berry

a spider sits in the corner of my room
with its heart stuffed full of death-beds
and earth and discarded shoes
and everyone else's geography

with hands holding tight
to the celestial backdrop
of flies and stench
it feeds its homely mouth

and prays that its buckle
of flesh will last out this night

with its belly full of webbing

with its head full of blood
the spider sings

and all night its hymn
is a measure of shocks
rocking this house

and all night I cannot sleep
hearing that stupendous pit
of beatitudes opening
wider and wider.

NORTH CRAG

I have come finally
to where the dead slag
falls mindlessly into the sea
where only a few nettles grip the hill-top
sending up their white flowers
into the salt-breeze

I have come to a mute room
to a mute finger pointing only slightly
to the far-off blue

here the sun doesn't brighten
the fog holds on to its vacancies

here age after age
the dull grey complexion of this crag
sits perfectly in the scheme of things
dieting on air

this is the first face of heaven
the first watchful turn of a head

this spit of land
is fostering a race
of sinewy bodies

the awakening rocks
taking on the eden-shapes of birds
and men.

RAT SONG

the rat is a bonfire
is a blaze of heavenly light
marooned among men

is a holy lamp
sent to brighten an unlit world

is a shimmering halo
sent to adorn the mountain

is a flaming lyre
sent to accompany the dead

is a burning path
sent to guide the righteous

the rat is a signal fire
ablaze on the earth
forever.

WORM SONG

weighted down with plumage the worm dances
like a prophet atop the mountain
like a swan through the darkness

never forgetting to crow out
the countless names of heaven
that gave him wings for this blackness

never forgetting the vortex of flight
carrying his lit face peacefully
beneath the bootsoles of men

always soaring from pole to pole
the whole earth an outreaching sky
carrying his diminished body
around the certain ecstasy
of this globe.

DEAD CROW AT GRAND LAKE

this landscape depends on a lank bird
depends on an installation of unmade flesh
on a wrongheaded body
                              positioned in the snow

these trees owe their initiative and grace
to this terminal eye
and burr of stagnant feathers

what would heaven be
without this blood-stained neb
resting on the globe?

what would the horizons do
lacking these wasted guts
to guide them on?

this rigid heart repairing the world.

LETTER FROM A JOURNEY

dear
the moon's bright cuſp
over the blueblack pool of water
over the red tongues
darting among the ſticks

we were here once before
in another time
in another shape
I remember your tail
your paws ſtruggling
with deſpair

the ſtars sat in the tree
the wind blew the music of duſt
remember?
me.

A SMALL PRAYER TO HEAVEN

O grimace of star on stone
O stony nightmare
mogging through our vacant hearts

O heartbreak covering the seafoam
covering the subsoil
covering the latitude of open air

do not disappear from our only eyes
do not leave us alone on the impassable earth

O earthlight shimmering in blood
do not forget our heads positioned
in the trees   our guts cushioning the mountains

O mountain kiss us once good-bye.

WAR IN AN EMPTY HOUSE

1982

A NETHERPOEM

in the basement where evening pulls in
the huge ropes of morning
where the sun fills the furnace red at nighttime

in the basement where the gramophone plays
the slow sound of the moon against the world
I came across an empty house
the empty rooms of your dark body

not the body you use now
but the other one
you didn't know existed

the body of a dwarf clothed
in handfuls of water

the little figure lying on the mineral floor

in the basement where the ocean originates
where the undersea mountains unfold into rain
where all the tides go to sleep without end
I heard the voice you never used

in the basement where all the fables come from
where all the stories smell of bandages
and spilled medication
where a riderless horse nudges
your folded body
I heard a voice that could
have been you

the missing words that sound like
a waterglass filled with footsteps
that are always coming back patiently
from the sea.

NOCTURNE

a beetle opens the door
a tuber closes the door

outside in the grass the keel of a dog
knocking against sleep
the crossbones of a rose
the wishbone of a spider
the rib of an empty space where nothing
grows that does not die first
with the simple passage of days

a moth moves
but is not yet born

a cat makes a web
beneath a stone.

DREAMTIME

in sleep there are many radios
turned to a station
where the death taxes are paid
where the Hittites perform their slow
unpleasant songs

in sleep there are many factories
where a Gnostic might work
measuring the humility of an egg

in the place where sleep comes from
where you and I come from
there is a seaside hotel
where Sumerians dance round
a bottle of dark medicine
where Kassites sit up all night
on rocking horses made out of thumbs

in the place where sleep comes from
where you and I come from so beautifully
there is a houseboat
filled with Babylonians falling in love
with the same old story about
your thick black hair

in sleep there are many diners
where Cathars drink the coffee your mother
made for you twenty years before

in sleep there are many trains
where Canaanites read your lost mail
where Bacchantes paint the clippings
taken from your long nails
where the radio on the empty seat
sighs once to itself

sounding like a strange church
sounding like a strange season
sounding like you.

PLEIADES

I was walking back barefooted
I was walking back to you
on the night I was born

there was a rust-coloured moon over my head
a sun-turned moon
changing the road into metal
into blue foil

to the left a black rain was falling
to the right a shower of gold was dissolving
a field of white stones
in front of me I carried gifts for you
in one outstretched hand
I held a bent nail
in the other a moth
they were the only suitable things
worth bringing into the world

on that night I could
think of nothing
I walked up a street
and walked back down it again

when I turned
my coat turned with me
to hear the wind
the voices driven past the moon
past the dull green leaves
on the half-finished tree

I felt small as a leaf
like the ghost of a hand
hem of a centipede
discarded inside a white cup

I placed a hand in my pocket
and felt the ocean moving
through my clothes
the fish   the round stones
the eight varieties of seaweed
common to this area

I took my new name
out of my pocket
and read it over once again

while up there
just above the rooftops
the moon and the wind
and seven dead girls
sitting on six burning chairs
spun slowly by

and with fourteen gloved hands
they were all pointing to you.

TARTAREAN WALK

for Jeannette

the moonlight falls to the ground in blue panes
and the dyke is almost real beneath our feet
as we walk out past the day
as we walk out past the night
with its one mystery inventing the sea again

this the underworld
where the dead pasture
eating the grey grass
between the rows of blue corn

but we are the real ghosts here
talking about our lives
and trying to name the net of constellations
that surround us forever

we are the real ghosts
wandering out along these dykes
and so in love with those stars
that we are almost asleep
almost absent from this place.

INSOMNIA

A fly appears on my book and I watch its enamel
tongue lick the page. In its eye I see all the
sleepers lying under the voices that a bee has
brought into the world. The fly has a furious
mind and yet holds the sleepers gently like a
string of bells that toll to themselves in a breeze.

GOD

the faded colour of two hands
operating a spider
over dry and deserted ground.

DEVIL

a thing of rags
a thing of death
a dry thistle that runs its hand
along a brickwall
looking for a place to sleep.

ARCHANGEL

an owl that suffers
from nightfall

from the silence
surrounding
a sheet of white paper
in an adjoining room.

PROPHET

a salamander
resting horizontally

between two red
and vertical fires.

MARTYR

a filament naked to the waist

a thread worn as a coat
by an invisible weight.

RETURNING TO SYDNEY

I stood in the doorway
entire evergreens were on my side
entire geraniums
who always seem to know my desires
desires which are always the weight
of a single owl burnt to a fine ash

I stood in the doorway
with a thin covering of algae
along my hand
the hand of rainy days
bouquet of fingers
turning the brass knob
of a starling
(a bestial growl)

I stood in the doorway
the tears in my pocket
purring softly to themselves
as the moon rose high
above the brown wooden house
where a bottletop lay
beneath a chair
in which someone sat waiting
for me all night long.

SYDNEY

this street I am walking
is where the iron-age dreams are kept
and the night lies anchored
between two phases of the moon
the bell in the tower
stuffed silent with bread

the street where I am walking
is the street where each car
is accompanied by a violin
where the graveyard is damaged by music

when I am here
I add up to water
to a cup where the water is fast asleep

when I am here
I am equal to windowsills
I am equal to fragments of earthenware
to pigeons feathered with silhouettes.

FROM

HAMMERSTROKE

1986

A SPIDER STANDING NUDE BEFORE A MIRROR

she was made in the shape of Rome
that city of spiders and the gods of spiders
and the spidery light of dead things
drifting down to paradise

how beautiful she looks
beside the broken world
and how graceful
drinking a moth or a fly
drinking the blood of the lamb

and the fortune she has
she has always had
in owning a home
that barely rises out of the shadow
of time or place
in owning a body
that lacks the sadness of a body

that lacks the hesitation of a body
made from a year of rain
and a burnt glove
from a pin
and the spiral heartbeat
of dust on water.

DOGS LIVE IN PLACES MORE SECRET THAN THIS

bees above the blood stream
in the garden
flies tasting the sunlight
on the wall
at night an angel's finger
among the moths

she can almost touch it all
she can almost smooth it out
like a fine sheet
of phantasmal skin
over a bed of bones and leaves

lying down beside her husband
she knows that dogs live
in places more secret
than this

that cave-fish
wearing their eye plugs
and swimming from placenta
to placenta
from abyss to abyss
have more to say to one another
have more to bless.

THE FARM AT FOUR A.M.

in the barn there are
two hogs hanging
from black ropes in the air

they are the old weights
the old judgements against us

in the kitchen there's a wife
I don't know whose wife she is
but in the dark grass of her body
an animal moves
to the swaying of her voice

in the well there's a moon
with its song of seven letters
the moon of the inner world
no one knows what it thinks
or what it will finally do

in the apple tree
there are four gods
the moth   the cloud
the dead child and the wind
with its blue mouth pressed
urgently against the leaves
as if it could speak
as if it could speak to anyone.

THE CORN GODDESS

you walk into a field at noon
a single flame dancing on your right shoulder
on your left a lazy column of blue smoke

the red tractor follows one during the day
the other at night

through the rows of corn
it takes its soul
(which is that small rupture
in the motor)
wishing to place it at your feet

it races after you all summer long
because in you it sees its mother
it sees the distant land of its birth

the land of abandoned horses
and terrifying winds

the land of iron wheels falling
out of the sky

if it wasn't for you
the tractor would find it impossible to breathe
in this new place
beside these men
these farmers seated comfortably
under these trees
eating apples that in any other world
would be on fire.

SNOWBOUND LETTER

it has snowed a lot since you were last here
the synagogue and the abattoir are covered in snow
the ships docked at the pier are white
the rapid pulse of the sailors can be heard at night
even this far inland
(like the snapping of dry twigs
in their arms and legs)

I'm not practical enough to live much longer
only a dozen more lifetimes or so
and then the freedom of insects again
the peace of being a fly for a thousand years

the window is open and it's cold in my room
but it's almost daylight and I'm listening
for the coal-train through the snow

this world separates us
with a single ache
with a button   with a grassblade
it takes so little effort
to keep us apart

the neighbour's lights have just come on
they're now removing the dry leaves and earwigs
from inside their mouths

it's the wind that shapes their lives
that fills the morning glass
with sugar and water

it's the wind that allows them to live
like birds on wires
pigeons that startle each other over breakfast

I can hear the train
although it's still miles away
soon I'll be able to sleep
soon I'll be able to put up my feet
to tie up my wrists and ankles
and pull the small black hood down over my heart.

ANTS TRANSFORM THE FATE OF COMMON MEN

the ants are on Cemetery Hill again
collecting the darkened faces
to curse them is pointless
they do God's work
cleaning the clay pit of breastbones and tiepins

they smell of lavender and almonds
and have eyes of watermarked paper
singing like castrati
high Kali-voices under the hill
cut apart by assorted winds

they live in a land of dry breezes over black spices
of insect pieces and handfuls of hair
in a nation of passageways
lined with that pink membrane from inside the mouth
in tunnels where heated shovels
are hung at every turn

when you drive to the city they bite into your hand
when you sit in your armchair they gnaw on your ring

ants transform the fate of common men
and those of queens and miners
and the Virgin of the Railyard tied to a stake
the night the great stars fell
like leaves out of a future tree

the ants tramp over the dead on dented legs
counting the pale fingers
and the equally pale eyes

you must learn to cherish their one secret
that foot-dance without fear or nausea
that exhausted motion among the bodies
the dry lips   the bruised tongues
the skeins of red ribbon unravelling
out of a torn side

caressing the soul (a sort of jelly)
stuck to the roof of the mouth

dragging tattered lungs and bowels
down black tunnels
to a mat of beef-red flowers
to the next green world.

tonight with the sea expanding
along the vibrations of one string
with the air smelling of amnesia and salt
Death moves gracefully as a temple doll
her porcelain feet over the round
and foam-covered stones

the child says:
"Death is the first star, she rises in the east.
She has followed me over burnt ground, she has
followed me into the world. I can hear her
thoughts. Those two kettles of boiling water, those
two tumblers of bees turning over and over in
the dark."

the sea fades and folds and fades again
the fog brings the miasmic smell
of rotting kelp and half-eaten fish
with silver cataracts over all their eyes

the child floats nervously upon the water
while among the rocks the night-birds cry out
making the sound of heavy keys
along a thin brass ring.

A POEM ALMOST WRITTEN AT
LE COUVOIR DE SCOTT, QUEBEC

the morning after their deaths
the chickens arrive back on earth
with photographs of God's hands
scotchtaped to their feet

they've been to Paradise
to the land of raw halos
and greasy violets

they've seen all the luscious blondes up close
and are swollen with sunlight

now they walk like heraldic animals
like helium-filled pigeons
perched on the edge
of their previous lives

and if we look closely
when they're in the yard
pecking at the dirt
we'll see among them the medieval sheen
of an invisible choir

the sweet bridal veil of the Otherworld.

OUROBOROS

for Renata

I

this gold snake could not sleep
its red self could not outrun
or its blue self mirror
even one single blade of straw
so it bit its tail
and rose into the polished air.

II

the ocean contains three pails of green water
and one of white
the air above that water
is made from dead combs and tridents
each square inch carries the colour
of a nail hammered into an unfinished wall
a snake holding a single thought
can live there forever.

III

a snake beside a moon
is flushed blue with memory
the memory of each vertebra
separated by light
a blue light allowing it to hold
onto the soft curvature of space.

IV

a snake bridled by its own tongue
shoed by its own mouth
has the brain of a horse
above the running waves
a horse carrying time
the infinity of hoofbeats
echoing down its own dark throat.

A FIRE AT BLUE BEACH

I keep the fire awake
with the sleep of twigs
and branches

beside the fire a rose
has grown
while I was off
gathering wood

I am wholly alone

the rose says so
by being red

the rose says
the wood I carry
is my own ghost
in my own arms

the rose says
the fire is death
and that it might
happen to me again.

FROM

WOLF-LADDER

1991

THE HITCHHIKER

the sky flinched
releasing owls to the circulation
to the never-endings between the trees

the moon rose like a dental chair
white and empty and smelling
of teeth torn from a liquid
from a mouth dressed in spills

he stood on the highway
a sad man
with a tobacco-stained anthill
for a heart

there was a city ninety miles away

a city at room temperature
on a November night

"I will learn," he said
"to endure hunger and the wind.
I will remember the voice I now hear
beside me. A voice made when Heaven and Hell
pass each other so closely they sound
like sticks and dry leaves rubbing
together in a ditch."

he was a sad man
and it was a clear night
so far from the city
that he could see the tangle of stars
above the firtrees
and the tangle of stars
was a climbing ghost
so old
that it creaked a little
in the darkness

"I will learn," he said
"to endure darkness and the creaking.
I will remember the voice I now hear
inside me. A voice made when Heaven and Hell pass
each other so closely they sound
like a man speaking to himself on an empty
highway."

he was a sad man
with a chest full of rain
and in his pocket
were two keys
that passed each other so closely   so cautiously
you could almost hear an address.

FEATHERED WINDOWS

your heart is a finger end
pushing itself into the sea

you stand in tall grass
littered with horse skulls
ant skulls
with stations of wind
burning under stones

the cold mist blown off the Atlantic
hits your face like minute wooden cubes

an owl flies overhead
his wings make the sound of doors
slamming behind him one by one
the doors of a great house
filled with morning light
feathered windows
black talons holding
the drapery and bedding
firmly in place

each room furnished
with the breath of a thousand sparrows
turning at once in the air

this is the house you will move into
the mansion of bone-white floors
and melting gardens
planted with ten thousand blue volts
of the purest air

where you can sit up all night
undisturbed beneath a sky of intersecting wings
the moonlight clotted between your fingers
the sea spilling out of its glass on the table
the coiled fountain
the clenched trees
the stars sounding like microscopic bells
thrown hard against the body.

is it a side street or a cat's jaw?
cerecloth or the body's flesh?
I've named it the heart's pillow
wind in a mirror   cloud-rope
lighthouse on the edge of a wound
beadwork   the mote's halo   wolf-ladder

I've called it both temple bell and medicine bed
sleep following the closing of doors
broom in a dusty corner
breath in a bottle
pin between the legs
beachstone   slow hammer
blood's seamless gesture

I've called it evening but I don't know
it could be the roach in the birthday cake
or the worm in the violin
or the snail on the highway
or the angel that carried the baby far away

tonight it's the murmuring sound
the predatorial sigh
twisted into a braid of flypaper and starlight
the cleft in the raindrop
the stove in the street
an eyelash at rest on a nail
a tongue ripening among oranges
on a windowsill
and oh yes   barking and barking
the company of dogs.

A FROZEN CLAIRVOYANCE

I

nothing moves in the icy street
nothing gathers up
what survived of memory.

II

I go walking
I go breathing the scent
of a frozen clairvoyance
the fiddlings of a planchette
frozen to the air
wondering whose dirty hands push
the frost along the window pane.

III

a thin snow circulates
round a furious child
a low fire burns the dead
each buried in their little stove
beneath the earth.

WOLF-LADDER

for Gwendolyn

> *an animal rests*
> *unaware of having been born.*
> —Jean Follain, The Evening Suit

Rung I: *Wolfache*

they sat up late   the hour on the table
she said: "Last night I heard a wolf howl
under the belted sky, howl and inhale
snow from a hand that looked exactly like
a world. And suddenly I thought, in Hell this
would be the sound made by petals falling on the grass."

Rung II: *Wolf at the Door*

"And tonight," he said, "the moon's in its fable,
the stars in their bag, there's a trout frozen
to a cloud, and the wolf's swampy breath
presses against the door. Its song drifting
through the house, its lunar bristles scraping
against the edge of things."

Rung III: *Dagger Woods*

"When I was a child," she said, "there were such
winds stirring those woods, such winds in the
hiding-places, in the earth's ear. I remember it,
the pigment of wolves blown violently through the
trees. I remember it, the fear across mended snow,
fear along my spine, like summer along a necklace."

Rung IV: *The Wolf Behind the Mirror*

he said: "This is the story I heard as a child.
That the spider fattens on wishes, the mouse on
tears, and the wolf eats the pretty mouth pressed
against the mirror and lives on that, and that alone."

Rung V: *Wolf and Rider*

"I've heard," she said, "that man and wolf
are one. Naked they ride out together,
their faces painted with ochre, their backs
dyed with henna. That they each desire the
same woman, long for the same full lips,
the same running hair. That what the man
loves the wolf must possess. That what the
wolf owns the man calls wife or sweetheart
or dearest blood. That she sleeps pearled
with stones. That it's an old story, coal-
scented and full of snow."

Rung VI: *Hearts and Tails*

he said: "My Grandfather told me the wolf's
heart is a gravesite passing back and forth
through a buttonhole, its eyes are offshore
lights seen through rain. That its hair is
our own darkest thoughts, its tail a braid
of three fears, one fear of the dark and
two fears of meeting a ragged stranger in
the street."

Rung VII: *In That House by the Rainy Sea*

"A wolf," she said, "is what remained of my Grandfather
after everything else had fallen into the abyss. A wolf
smelling of wet campfires and old bedding, standing in
that house by the rainy sea, in the cool morning of the
kitchen, weeks after his death. My Grandmother called him
husband and rubbed his body with camphor oil. To her a wolf
is a ghost stuffed with fur and teeth. To her a wolf is
simply a lover who has stumbled over the edge of the world."

Rung VIII: *Prayers Through the Leaves*

"Sometimes," he said, "I hear the wolf's prayers far away
through the leaves. They're like the tearing up of planks
from the bottom of a ship at sea, like a cauldron full of
blood and snow boiling away on a halo. Each time I hear this
I think that the god of wolves must be the god of men. That
priests must also live among them, dogs from the towns who
preach of a god made wholly of scraps from a table. That wolves
like men long for the same bowl of water, the same dish of
meat placed under the shining stars."

Rung IX: *The She-Wolf*

she said: "Every so often a wolf calls from under
the table, from behind the pictures hung like planets
on the wall. If she were a dream I would wake up. If
she were a person I would escape through sleep. She's
like an insect boring into a wooden box in which you
have slipped your body hoping for paradise or at least
the darkness of six trees. I heard her one night from
her lineage behind the snow. It snowed in parables, in
blessings, as if the sky were a cathedral of stars and
chalk. As if that wolf was a sister of the painful vow,
a nun quietly tearing at her beads."

Rung X: *The Wolf-Road*

"Sometimes," he said, "I watch the stars float back
at dusk across the waters and hear the wind's cloth
bell in the hands of a beetle. Then I long for what
the grass knows in their ten million towers under the
trees. I long for the wolf-road where the grass walks
and the beetle names the hour and the wolf carries the
torn half of a moon between his teeth. This is my burden,
my ration of shadow, to always feel like a man who's about
to wake from sleep and put his first footprint on the earth."

Rung XI: *Wereland*

"My wish," she said, "is to discover the body of an
evening between the trees. And parting the hair of
that body to find, one by one, a pack of wolves and
the sleepers that run with them through the woods. I
want the evening that casts the shadow of a howl every-
where. I want elsewhere. Wereland. The wolf-eared
corner where two worlds meet. I'm tired of sadness,
of emptiness, I insist on a wolf anointing me in the
blood of a knife cut by water. I long for my hands coming
back to me out of the earth with a burning candle on
every finger, each as sharp as a claw."

Rung XII: *Words from a Drawing*

he said: "Wolves pass through needles tonight. The snow
collects on a voice tonight and the darkness has drawn a
man and woman seated at a table. Outside, a deep forest of
chairs and tables bends in the wind. In this drawing we're
talking about wolves and someone's listening, writing it
all down. The wolves themselves are like dust at a wedding,
like ashes poured from a star, no one sees them. The wolves
move one step ahead of stones, they circle the eye. No one
has ever seen or heard them, not even us with our stories
studded with teeth, wrapped in fur. As if we were two travellers
with all our possessions carried in the body of a wolf
lashed to our backs, to those ghost-licked shapes, those solid
and unpainted spaces between the sounds."

AN OLD AMPHIBIOUS GOD

I

Words Engraved On a Bead

not the Devil's diligent finger
pointing out of the ground
or out of a pinetree

not the roach sliding down
Death's greasy back

or the angel drawn from
its sheath of burning skin
or Jehovah weighing each act
moistened by a soul
not the saint nailed
to a screendoor
on a summer's afternoon

but the god of drowned mouths

the god of lost hands
with his rosary of flies

an old amphibious god
a pre-world divinity
that leans upon the blood.

II

His Return

he came out of a rainspout
out of a cipher
out of the idea of two accidents
facing each other over an abyss

he came out of
the grass of a continent
turtle-faced
newt-legged
red-backed like a salamander
walking on moss
always walking on moss

and when he spoke
it was so much like dry earth
like a moon-shut town
like the mind bending
over its own fierce
and cornered voice
a cat-plated voice
a crying out among
mountainous shapes
the past calling out
among wooden beds
shoved up against the sea.

III
Anatomy Notes

his eyes   the hush and stitch of two pins.

his mouth   the pond's full weight.

his nose   the tip of a mouse.

his heart   the wind under a chair.

his lungs   saddles ridden by two brides.

his arms   washes of milk.

his hands   two bricks a minute before nightfall.

his ribs   coffin slats.

his torso   rags tied with water.

his belly   the jailer's halo.

his cock   smoke in a sleeve.

his legs   tooth-marks.

his feet   the sound of blood and curls on a pillow.

IV

A Few of His Proverbs

(1) I pick up the wolf by its tooth
the amoeba by its tail
and the man by his word.

(2) what is paradise
but a gold table
floating above a dirt floor
and all of this
covered in clouds.

(3) an axe is a piece of wood
with a scream fastened to one end
a man is a piece of flesh
with a storm fastened to one end
sometimes they meet at night in the street.

(4) what is the human soul
but a claw pointing back
to the forest.

(5) the stroke of a pen dipped in ashes
the cut of a knife across a shadow
these are only two of my signatures.

(6) every sparrow deserves
a soldier's funeral
every man deserves
a water-filled ditch
the rain's grave.

V

Naming Him

add his name to the world
maybe it can be spelled out
with sticks and bits of broken glass
with a nail driven into
an embrace
with a worm carried under
the tongue
with a hundred books
burning against a wall

maybe he has a name
given to him by
the black beetle
that lifts the dead
above the grass
so they can see

by hilltops   by harbours

by paths painted on the earth

or perhaps in the end
his name is just that tattoo of rain
engraved on his left shoulder
rain drifting into a woman's yawn
like so much shadow
like so much belief.

VI
A Confession

I don't pray to him
but give back what is his
this swampy brain
wholly swamp and carrion wall

I ask him for nothing
but merely lift up the stones
at my feet
simply swallow this small fetish
of flesh and water

I ask him nothing
but throw the darkness
from my pockets
and stroke this icon
of raised skin on wood

skin of mirrors
mythy wood of poorest danger
with its round scents
of straw and blood

the smell of far off
voices on the breath.

THE BIRTH OF METEORS

the mosquito-god
(Conqueror of Worlds)
turns mosquito after mosquito
over onto its back
which sets each one bleating
into the firmament
like a lamb

as the day wears on
and the amusement recedes
the mosquito-god's fingers
tire and fade to stars
and finally to pinpoints of darkness

dead stars falling
eventually
into crevices of rain
into the nights of sleeping men.

THAT GIANT SILVER BALL

it's always best
to put the gun directly
against the heart
only then can you see the darkness
you promised yourself
a million years before

pull the trigger
and out of the barrel
comes the edge of a forest
where the city becomes so thin and pale
it washes out among the blades of grass

a footstep beyond the grass
is a wilderness of spruce and pine
lit by a half-moon
no larger than a hen

you are a long way from time and space
yet the trees continue to grow
and you walk among them

what's new between the trees?
a flutter of moss?   a wolf
with the eyes of a schoolgirl?
a rabbit's head asleep in a stone?
a dead mouse clotted round
a sprig of wormwood?

maybe only the dog is new
a fifty pound dog that follows
you patiently into the forest
holding a bullet between his teeth

perhaps after death that's the only change
this fly-black dog padding along behind you
holding the bullet where your blood
continues to look for arteries   for angels
for the next version of your heart

which is a feather buried in a bog

which is a nest of spidershit
and sorrel leaves

which is that giant silver ball
the martyrs toss to each other
when they are about to breathe in that
last mile of fire and flesh
on a windy hill.

REPEATING THE DREAM

continue   go at it again
black clouds   smoking earth
a marsh at night
the shock of your own footsteps
fingernails holding on tightly
to the moon

what was it you said
about the city?
oh yes   you could see the city
and it was far away
highrises filled by a single breath
little shops buried under pine needles
wolves asleep in cars

the city was far away
but you weren't walking
toward the city
you were on your way
to the sea
to the wind   the crashing waves

you heard something beneath
the water
that sounded like a tongue
moving slowly inside a heart
like lightning calling and calling
from under a tablecloth
and you followed into the tide

now you turn to me again
saying what a strange dream it was
asking what it means
asking if you are dead or alive

again I put my cup of morning coffee down
on the bright windowsill
again I lean forward
and say I love you mother
I love you dearly and you are dead.

ANGELS OF DEATH

they entered the house at evening
on the roof there was a ladder of birds
on the lawn the slow spin of star on gravel

there was the scent of folding chairs in the air

a hundred entered single file   shoeless   rags
in their mouths

they entered with only the furniture to meet them
the lamps and tables leaning like violets
into the remaining light

a hundred sat down in the darkness
their faces were covered in smoke and leaves
their bodies were just a drawing of bodies

one picked up a slice of bread
the others watched the little wheels
spin round inside it
the fields of wheat   the long roads of dust

they each held a syringe filled with a voice
they each held an axe by its leg
they waited for two years in the kitchen
but you never returned

this is to let you know
I sat with them for those years
and now it's safe to come back

that they're gone   that they found work in the city
that the syringes now fly with sparrows
that the axes are all married to knives
and live quietly deep in the forest

that you can come home   anytime

that you'll live forever.

THE FUTURE HAS GATHERED EVERYWHERE AGAIN

I put on my coat (the weight
of hair and nails) and go outside
with my legs covered in dust
and the barking of dogs

a number of worlds circle
overhead in the dark
a number of planets brimming over
with stones and lighted threads

my hands are bloodshot
from lack of sleep
from building a black bed
when they should be sleeping

from the street comes a prophecy
driven into the last drops of rain

the future has gathered everywhere again

before this night is over
I will write something on a piece of paper
in the morning it will sound
like a kitchen tap being turned
by a breeze from the garden
like a shoe
like the lowing of newborn insects
left spinning above the trees.

DEAD DOG: BRAS D'OR 1962

flesh sogging through bone
teeth profiled in seepings
the yellowing tongue
more scut than tongue
in a swanskin mouth

light-swallower
meeting an evil end
at the end of a road

breathtaker smeared with a rush
of wormy combs
through your hair

bone-drinker incised
a thousand times
by a maggot's tidal sigh
by a beetle's grieving saw

I remember you still
after all these years
as a cauldron boiling over
in the grass
and the witch who set
you going
waiting
still waiting even now
for that rough and cradled soup
to be done to a bead
to a drop
to a pock of purest dew.

STATIONS OF THE LEFT HAND

1994

DRAGON

the man sat clothed in shade
bearded in hymns
reading his copy of the earth
making promises to the grass

at his feet a salamander moved sleep
a little further onto land

a spider drank her black syllable
from both worlds once again

the ferns in the shadows laboured
to turn their mind
their single drop of blood
to a single thought

the man sought the comfort of belief
sought the old word in the grass
with its bone-coloured heart
its candle-scented eyelids
its few brush-strokes of skin

the man read from
his copy of the earth
but a new word came
to sit on his shoulder
like a feline-bird

like an enormous cat
with feather-studded fur

its eyes tapered to red
its hands big with holding

its ears   its wings
its braided back
all mottled with graces

the grace of sleep upon wood
of idea upon stone
the grace of the appointed cloud
in the appointed breeze
bringing its coppery rain

and the man reading
the rain in his book
smiled at the word on his back

that unaffected flying cat
that terrible wingless bird
which like the serpent in the
grass of the book
stirred and stirred
and crackled in blue.

BENEATH THE ISINGLASS

for Chris Dewdney

amoebae prowl and chart the flesh
circumnavigate the talus
in a year
cross the great province
of lungs in ten

they brought news to Novalis
a vortex to lust
a socket of angels
to the mind

they speak of tides often
the tidal pourings of boundaries
into the blood
they speak of Epsilon Boötis
thickened with the moss's breath
craggy pyramids
of morning   noon and night
two hundred and thirty
light years away

they're the same as our hands
            our glum faces
            our lips
drinking water from a cup

but they're not human
not nearly human
more like swans in our bodies
blue swans adrift
on their sides under thunder
swan-shapes flattened thin
by the pressure of constant sight
of being seen without end
by an unblinking god

not the god of amoebae
who has stopped just now
beneath the isinglass
of countless stars
stars bristling
with maelstroms and hobs
that god is motionless
yet at the same time
he is nodding
with cheeks full of ascidia
he is waving
from far off
over the newly fallen snow.

URSA MAJOR

you will walk along the path
with the hour's tricolour in your hair
flag of time in its bright and swaying vertigo

you will walk a long while
between predator-stained pools
and rocks transpierced with sight
before noticing bats flying
like miniature oxygen tents
through the air
the surf of the Milky Way
lost among pines
a fox lit from within
by one bare bulb
like an interrogation room

you will walk till you find
a pack of migrant stones
resting for the night
around a braid long
buried in the earth

turning left through a grove
of maples
you will come upon a small lake
above which will hang an alembic moon
and further off a single cloud
resting its white pelt
on some trees

soon a bear will arrive
a star-collared bear
with feet of ancient rubble
and arms belted tight
with small strokes of fire

you will give him your hand freely
and without fear
then he will lead you
deeper into the medicine-dark forest
to meet your dead family

your father superimposed
on a framework of gnawed branches
the wrappings of your mother
seated with her hands erased
your sister bundled in parings
of light

you must not touch them
or they will crumble to a drizzle
of salt and ashes
to various levels of scarring
to threadbare webs
clinging to ankles of grass
wet with the spider's breath

you may exchange words
which will appear to you
as cubes of ice
or black straw levitating
through the air

after an hour you must return
with that rough and solemn bear
who will ask only a kiss
in return for his guidance
not the kiss of charity
or obligation
but the kiss of lust
and the nuzzling of your breasts
the sibylline kiss of strangers
the pubis-ridden kiss
which is all that can ever
bring you back to the living world.

THE ANTLERED NIGHT

hunter return from the land of hunting
wake to a fleeting and sudden pain
as if a diaphanous brick
passed through your heart

wake with musk and blood on your pillow
say the grass had been a hunting-grass
following the deer as it did
deep into the mossy woods
hounds of grass and bride-fed clouds
all pointing to a stag among the trees
the hive-encrusted trees

hunter   mouser
point your moonlight
at your own ghost
fire into that prevailing spook
behind your eyes
it's a stag and a man
and a massive forest

huntsman the world is green
in seconds   in minutes
it's a green and yellow light
in an hour it's all carpenter's wood
from petal to horizon

awake hunter
you don't fool anyone
with that sad pavane
among the trees
listen to your sleep in the wind
your pillow made of chaos
granular breath and falling earth

deerstalker awake
feel the stag-driven wind
around your bed
the antlered night sticky
with something fatal and underfoot
the earth underfoot is both pillow and sleep
sleeper and every bed

huntsman put down your gun
and listen to the ferns cry out
from their rags and beaks
to the trillium cry out
with a thundering X
to mark the thunder of the spot
where you'll be reduced
to the radius of an anatomy
a skull many-headed
by degrees of absence
by an eyeful of furious leaves.

RIVER PIECES

for Malcolm Ross

   *

clouds creak in the sky
herons creak in the sky.

   *

the dark approaches itself
from all sides once again
the moon lifts
its white and gravelled head
out of the hills.

   *

the river holds ghosts
that have thickened
into salmon.

   *

on its banks
weeds grow into children
far away
from their parent's door.

*

an oak tree beside the water
pulls up the shadow of a house
that once stood here
or one still to be built
room after room
up through its roots.

*

to walk beside the river
the long walk of the body
is a threshing of shadows.

*

to stand by the river
is to hear words beginning
in the hands
starting as indelible amnesias
being forced up through the hands.

*

to listen to the music of the river
is to hear a final music
a silk-hedged current
transfixed by a mirror
and a placing of leaves
over the eyes
the age of an evening
over the eyes.

NIGHT-SEA-JOURNEY

these worms are moments
of a former earth
yet I do not expect them to tell time
like the chiselled breath of prayers
across an ascending hawk tells time

what I want from worms
is their rowing in the flesh
their cold little boats
their eyes of smudge
their mouths like mailslots

I want their night-sea-journey
across darkened water
with their captain shouting
over the rushing waves

I do not expect to understand
but to call from land
from their bruise-coloured beach
a few words they might
take with them to that far shore
of bones and stars
of miracles and bliss.

BRIDE AND GROOM

for Heather Dohollau

bats in their Dantean circles

full moon at its oaken door

the centuries burnt low
to the ground

coyote-bride through a black field
her groom and their stoking-faiths
the furnace of touch and smell
the hackles of a flame

people once lived here
but now there are only eyeholes
where the people once stood
only tongues
where their words were spoken

beyond this breathable field
beyond that sack of trees
the cliffs drop their innumerable claws
one by one into the sea

bride and groom live here now
light their way with a burning hair
on the tip of each ear

eat the earth   the sheep
the rabbit in the earth

call men and women out
of their deaths
to sit with them through
the long night

for the wedding night is also lonely
love and the spilling of blood
a sadness

when the sea is so still
and the moon over the sea

when there are no other
brides or grooms
on the face of the earth

when weddings and their shapes
have all passed away.

TRANSMIGRATIONAL POEM
(GARTER SNAKE AT ARISAIG)

how often have we crawled
out of the amuletic
configurations of the grass

with glass teeth
and a gold-filling for a mind

how many times did we place
our invisible arms
around a heated day
as if it were an egg
warmed by a midden
of complexions
by a handful
of glittering scales.

TRANSMIGRATIONAL POEM
(RED FOX ON NORTH MOUNTAIN)

how often have we been
that red book in the green forest

how many times did our words
run through the blood
till they were wild enough
to print
till they were pious enough
to print

those pages turning
in the bindings of a tooth.

TRANSMIGRATIONAL POEM
(BALD EAGLE OVER HORTON BLUFF)

how often have we flown
in those drafty feathers
circling in all twelve skies
of the clock
the clock folding time
behind us as it moved.

STATIONS OF THE LEFT HAND

to the memory of Joshua Julian Barnes

1 *The Wall of Slaps*

in this bare place
with the sea exhuming
the sea from the mind

with gulls
who are only partly
the dirty bleachings
of the pearled and shaken air

with sharks
who are all grey thumbs
torn from invisible hands
hands that at least once
fall suddenly and softly
through our blood

in this bare place
with tyrannical brines
and salted trees
in all these
exterior raindrops
lost to interior fires
there is no end of faith
to watching the ocean
tear its own shadow loose
from those rocks
from that wall of slaps

the shadow of a pasture
outstretched under lambs
deepened by wolves
and supernovas and deeper lambs

which is the shadow of the mind
peeling away
being pulled away
stubbornly from the earth.

6 *Fiery Searcher*

there's not enough sunlight
not enough breeze in the light
but that's what crying is for
tears scented with pine-needles
and cobwebs
rocks whimpering on rocks
and moss too
filled with a sorrow
that knows no sacrament
no end that isn't moss
holding onto an absolute of otherness

so when the Fiery Searcher comes
with the tolls of a beetle
with the stride of a beetle
with its beetled instances
and eyes black as dead chocolate
you notice a change

what was invisible remains invisible
but now all are celestial
off-shoots of leavings and dust
of a heeltap in a glass

now the sun is six-legged
dazzling as labra and antennae
against the skin

a beetle is a beetle
or a phantasm in armour
but notice how the beatific nudge
is felt through the wood
how stones lash themselves
to the moment

it may be a coincidence
but it's a beetle-coincidence
a bug-abstraction
only a second or two long

it was for this second
of time only
that the spires reached
promising themselves
something beyond
a martyr's chromatic wounds

this is why the church was built
why the plate of bright coins
floats down the isle
without a bride

an insect is the equal
of any god
because any god is simply givenness
brought to our attention

so why not a beetle
this Fiery Searcher
the crown fits
burns   smokes
like the chimney
of a ferocious and particular star.

EPIPHANY UNDER THUNDERCLOUDS

each night I spend whatever
God made during the day
spend it freely
on paper and empty air

I spend because God is only
a resemblance of God
only a conjuring built out
of nebulas and wheat
by a few old men
asleep in their escapes

I believe in God
because those old men
sleep among paintings
they've never seen
because they're part
of the paintings
little dabs of colour
with stern faces
and arms akimbo

while these men were awake
and walked about in the world
their bodies were easily
corroded by any movement
of flesh in the street
they were terrified
they were as weak as sleeves
and God knew He was
as many arms
that filled them
with a total weight

God doesn't exist
and that was His best idea
to keep it simple
as every priest knows
reality ebbs away by noon

so better to have
the rolling embrace
of being invented
like the wheel
which carries the silence
in baskets up the hill

I spend whatever God makes
because He doesn't exist
and will never miss it

I believe in God
because I'm paid so well
so often

also I believe because
I'm saddened by belief
saddened by praying hands
by the little footsteps
that hurry back and forth
beneath the storm.

A BRIEF HIEROLOGY AMONG A FEW TREES

Vesuvius   stigmata
Crab Nebula
such unmoored wounds
adrift in time

I pray to spiritous dogs
to candles growing wild
in the grass

instead of memory
stars fill the air

God is a stallion
(the colour of discarded boards)
racing towards an extended hand
in the darkness
ten thousand miles away.

TO A NUMINOUS PRESENCE

namegiver   jawbreaker
helmsman you have once again
guided the night
safely out of wounds

now close your eyes
put out your hands
this is when
the aftertaste of heartbeats
is bought and sold

when thinking is chafed
by breathing slow

in your right hand
I'll place a mistake
in your left a fear
of eloquence

if you drop one
the day will begin
if you drop both
we'll all sleep peacefully
the sleep of paper
hearing only your name
if it is spoken
and the cricket's blue telegram
among the weeds.

PICTOGRAPH

1

I stand in an alley where all the stones lie
like broken wrists in the earth

a morning in September and this space between buildings
like the far end of a hospital ward
where faces gather in corners
before departing from the world

here an entity of formless duration inspirits
the place with sorrows that push against light
weeping being the oldest hymn   most ancient song
it stands and breathes among the apparitions you never see
legions of lost and possible shapes   the crowd half-spoken
scrivened on air   plainly visible to flesh but not mind
or eye secure in its watery resemblance to rain on good sleep.

2

there should be pictographs along these walls
as there are sometimes at the bottom of deep canyons
ones of spirits dancing
holding onto their green tongues with both red feet

this is a dry riverbed where a presence touches you
with the pastiche of considerable nothings
a presence like someone holding a ton of wilted flowers
an inch above your head and you sense that weight
and a voice is speaking and unspeaking in turns
saying and crackling and wishing to be near.

THE PASSAGEWAY

the mind is emptiness or almost so
no more than the small space between
the horse's shoe and dry soil
no less than the gallop of a horse
across clefts of nothingness
under birches that lead to the river

the salmon in the river are almost so
still you hardly notice them holding open doors
decorated with venerable black gills
doors that breathe
that lead down into the earth

the passageway has no room for the mind
or the body with its needlepoints of sorrow
these must be left behind like clothes on a riverbank
along with the horse who knows the way so well

what's left of you must travel
like the child asleep in its mother's arms
but you're not sleeping
and you're no longer a child
you're a lamp through which fire passes
but you see no light   feel no heat
which means you're coming close
upon something that's motioning to you
down there in the darkness

it could be a swell of teeth
it could be a stranger or an enormous storm
or the deepest word that knows nothing of pity
or your struggles with loss and desire

whatever it is you've been carrying it all your life
and must finally meet its gaze
eyelids that opened the moment you were born
when you rose up into the world

eyes that are creatures in themselves
that are slayer and slain
scream and whisper
all the shadows lying down.

WHAT THE BESTIARY SAID

after many sorrows and thoughts broken
body pains and blows to the heart
after living in poorer lands
with human company in every mirror
I remembered what the bestiary said
and allowed the deer of the slender sadness
to take my voice and my hearing
the wolf of the impenetrable eyes
to remove my flesh and bone
the salmon to take my spirit
and I lay on lichens worn clean
by whispers close to the ground
so that I was the nothingness there
with only the beetle's breath to carry me till morning.

DRAGONFLY

my wings barely reach into the outer world

I dart through the swarm entangled in Eros
picking hearts like straws out of their bodies
picking blank eyes off such grinning faces
tearing out the sexual interiors
hinged all along their backs

I eat because the inner world
wants some longing at the crossroads
some hunger in the wingspan

three millimetres above the pond
is where you meet the gods coming through
clad in threads   in millions of deafening scratches

I bow down before them   I'm so many jagged points
along a second of ecstasy
I'm so many dark crowds visible unto death.

OWL

the timberline is all driftwood
floating in from the millennium
the bogs search for pleasures
that only a mother could provide

I'm a few feathers and a clock face
the presence of clasped hands in the tree
of a fist succeeding in the democratic air

each of my wings is a district that knows of no other
I'm carried along by the suspension of disbelief
holy   holy   holy
it's silent and dark and the shadows are rising
the spirits of bears lift the trees
mice follow me into the air.

THE FOX AFTER DEATH

there are silk climbs
and burlap climbs
places for me to go

as the spider goes
but with the sense of joy
a thousandfold

shine after shine
is the only way to describe death
bloodshine untranslatable
and flesh like clouds in the distance

having once been a fox
I flow like a river now
inside flinches of light
this must be the way
to the present
to an animal place
a dry field
that slowly pushes
its sticks into God.

OSPREY AND SALMON

wings extended   gliding

dark pulse suffering fields of light

inside it all the mirrors fall silent
no images are cast   no sun or clouds
no threshold opened or closed

morphology of pure form
pinions that shudder against oblivion

it watches cream-coloured eyes at the water's edge
eminence of wadded feet along the shore
grottoes in a shell   mangers in a death
drifting on foam   bodies uncreated
among columns of reeds

the world arrives just as it descends
centuries return to their positions
along empty space

it dives towards the water
a fall withdrawn into eyesight

the salmon is astonished to find
that its fins will concede to the spirit of other things
that its gill openings hold all the names of God
deity and being
the full white solitude of death.

A GRIEVING MAN

the priest's house is made of feathers   black feathers
with dry blood down the shafts

outside grasshoppers lie still in the weeds
and on the stone steps a grieving man waits
blue lice in his hair
like a horse's mane blue with starlight

he carries messages from Death
both elbows have small wings like hummingbirds
his teeth are flesh   his hands bone
he's in league with all that's holy

the grasshoppers all hold wafers in their mouths
they're old churches without congregations
and are ready at any moment to leap clear of the earth.

SENTIENT BEINGS

in the abattoir after closing hours
when the walls and floors
smell sweet as taverns
warm as bedrooms where children sleep
when the fifty meat cleavers and the two hundred knives
hang from wooden pegs shining
like ice skates
and bloodied aprons are no longer flags
hung at all the entryways of death
you hear a whisper distant and alone
no crying any longer   no sobbing
no piercing screams obstructing the ceiling fans
just this rustling of a tongue
between two dry leaves in a corner somewhere
a feather between two stones

and the whisper is like a salamander descending
an immense staircase on such small legs
that the fatigue almost makes it stop

the whisper is our longing
for the inner eyes of the predator
teeth of the insectivore
a herbivore's composure
all the marine animals we wish we were
birds that simply fly away
those invertebrates that mate with a flame
inside their deepest selves
those larvae that need and know of nothing
but the earth's hold on duration

it asks "Where is the total weight
of being alive?"

it asks "Where are all the dark paths that lead
our lives astray?"

LYNX

I have come to the Land of Forms
because there are others like me
we come to imagine ourselves

because snow is half the body
belief half the mind

our feet are soft dark ears
faithful hearing of faithful loss
we listen with the roots of trees
the rabbits ripen   ripen and fall to earth
we approach making them red with predestined wounds
the quiet sequences   the great turbulence
among the sounds that wish to be.

THE INVENTION OF PALMISTRY

the owl sleeps   giving off sunlight
far below on the forest floor
red ants build
one black needle for the length
of white thread they found in the road
there are no tailors among their kind
no garment makers
their master is the farmer's daughter
the grunting girl
the suffering one
she will sew for them
they will take her below
this voice of summer
this youthful hope
she'll backstitch and hemstitch
and seam the deepest worlds
she'll meet Death in their tunnels
and sew for his hands a line of destiny
a line of fate and a line of heart
and along his eyes the lines of laughter
but not the line of life which would anger him

she'll rule there as queen
and fill slowly with honey
and Death will pass them by
Death will read his fortune in the stitchings
of such moments that are his hands
and pass them by.

LOCKS AND KEYS

the dead man lies in a field beside a river
weeds study the sky   stars crackle in the crisp air
a bear comes and lays its head on his chest
an angel comes to count his eyelashes one last time
an otter comes to choose from the man's memories
a recollection that suits it best   one without thirst or hunger
something sweet to take back to its dark waters

the dead man has a key in his pocket
the lock is two hundred miles away waiting for his return
from deep inside there's a slight whispering
the turning of a key that isn't there
tongue in the mouth that mustn't speak up
not in this dreadful place   this world
where doors never open by their own accord

the dead man now sees that the passageway
to the next world is made of peace and axe blows
woven so tightly together it feels like flesh against the spirit
but any lock knows this prayer of travelling
any key could point you in the right direction
any doorway could tell you where the new day begins.

CHILD OF THE EARTH

1

at evening the musk of falling snow reaches the earth
snow that will fall all night   turning round in pivots of space
spaces centred on moonlight   the moonlit ridges
of the self that abounds

so many selves make up the nightly routines   so many
fall with the snow upon the land   drown in the wintry sea

the body sits and the snow drifts down at light's end
the self drifts into woods and hills
arriving long after the world was made
the dark somewheres already in place and folded
as if time had passed   folded as you suppose it would be
if you arrived late to sit alone among the trees
among the cool embraces   the awayness of snow.

2

sitting in the woods you think of other worlds
planets where snow also falls   sulphur snows   iodine snows
the arsenic snows of Saturn   neptunium snows
toothed hills filling with empurpled flakes of neon
this great depth of distances is comforting
among pine trees who have no inheritors but themselves
beside the river frozen to a strength
that would break if it moved
and you think of things that you can't bear without shadows
leaning in upon your flesh   all the semblances leaning there.

3

snow heals the moment's burn
which is bright as Alpha Cygnus
of fixed position   of infinite birth
of indissoluble address
heals the wound that secretes its appetite upon you
knives that shave solace below the flesh

you sit as snow drops past the meridian
past the cuffs of trees
down among the inscrutable levels
to atoms forgetting reality
to a bare place where all visible things appear
as shades if they appear at all
ghosting around the emptiness
calling the elements home to their beds
home to every harm left unattended
a winter that surrounds you   seeable among the trees.

4

for many lifetimes the snow fell and you were the stillness
positioned there
you were the mechanics of snow and twisted ends of stars
structures of the self growing and fading into birth

O child of the earth you are me and us and the rabbit
who has believed longer than we have   purling evocations
in his warren like blood moving through its tunnels
seeking the backs of our legs   the palms of our hands
the movement it feasts upon   the edible motion

you're the pond pushing life out from its centre
cord grass drunk along the shore   bees pouring out of amber
all this which is part of the self   the cool of the night
the fire behind us we rarely see   quietude
you're the ocean setting forth   the first stone it touches
the wind that will blow the snow away
blow your particles into empty space   O empty space
this is the self   all worlds   the single place.

FROM

ALL OUR WONDER UNAVENGED

2007

WALKING DOWN TO ACHERON

1

I walk along a road leading down to the river
underfoot hieroglyphs from the Devonian Age
sealed tightly in flat grey stones   overhead
clouds ease back from the horizon   into one
continuous shadow of Destiny's resolve

a cool day in June   house finches handing out the sky
the earth lying like a grain of wheat in a great barn
                    the moon whispering under straw

a light drizzle keeping time with the pollen
coyotes wandering the hills   God in their legs

how quietly the senses move between the pine trees
like vapour through the needling of light.

2

I remember last summer finding a pond near here
spending an afternoon watching dragonflies hover
their every heartbeat fastened with pins
one to the next to the final one outside the world

I knelt down and touched the water   barely
like an old appointment scarcely kept   the surface
pulse of the pool pushing back against my fingers
which I knew was you   dead and set to music
you in a hymn darkly spread   away and placeless

I recalled that part of the Heart Sutra where it says
The infinitely far away is not only near, but it's infinitely
near. It's nowhere, and nowhere it is not. I was certain
I could live with that   just that and the tension of water
                                        against my fingertips.

3

today there's the walk to the river   rounded corners
of the phantasmal   the shifting plurality of matter
rocks and trees   the brassy oaths of grackles
the subsoil underslung with the respiration
of Heaven   foxes with amulets ribbing their physiques
luck of spring and full bellies   and my small ghost
making its way through
                  continuously emptying flesh into breath

today there's my shadow on the summits of dandelions
on damp weeds   on the figureheads of stumps
there's the ache that goes before me   wraithing
around turns in the path   that desire for deliverance
the soul's nudge   that little jinx in the body

a good idea to ignore it   to look the other way
watch granite boulders dog-eared in the earth
count the trees   the fallen ones   about to fall still
further into Acheron and be carried away like mist
acknowledge the tamarack clotted into flower
the plantain   all the grasses of no fixed address

notice the sun's appearance over the treetops
over each darkness turning in its resting place
over the far-off sound of the river maffling
like the voices of the ancients sealed in hives
open-mouthed   a fathom down in the honey.

4

a good time of day to attend to all the details
keep an eye on the clouds holding their great fires
notice the days curled up in the tracks of deer
watch a pair of mourning doves walk back and forth
along the banks of the river   like two lame girls
stopping at intervals to circle the absence of a third

it's that third dove the soul is always seeking
some part of us always looking for what can't be seen
                              what won't be revealed

I'll take comfort in the river coursing along its stones
flowing east through its fetishes   faded embraces
miming connections at the eddies   doubling back
on themselves like thought   every vortex thinking clear
as bright water   speeds polished by atom-fall through
the crossings   their circuits of pure light

I'll console myself with the flowering-rush growing
along the shoreline   with its rhizomes in deep nativity
with speckled trout steadying themselves in the current
each fin a hunch that the world is still there
each move of their tails a doubt   a push of suspicion

I'll take solace now in this snail intersecting my path
its horns pressing into the solitude of God   just there
where it hurts   where grief begins.

5

I'll sit here with slender kingdoms for awhile
with the planetary houses of seeds and pollen
to watch the river take on its serpent form
bringing forth an old sleep
from the bottom of things   things darkened
by a little light   heartbreakingly visceral
the luminous unseen threading through

meanwhile above me wasps enter and leave
their paper convent   Sisterhood of the Vespids
their contemplations severe
their shine leaning down into their dark eyes

other insects drifting about like ash-keys
wings hitched to whispers coming
from over the horizon
                    lifting them along
carrying them through the algebra
which we're always certain never adds up

I'll sit with arithmeticians in the moss
millipedes and the red-backed salamander
wait with them for the hour that comes eventually
to un-number things   to unthink the grand design
quietly as the sound of time settling into pearls
or paper pavilions unfolding just inside the mind

at moments like this I think of the Underworld
you seated there on your silver chair
all the walls stuffed with beards from the prophets
to keep in the sounds   all that longing
all those goodbyes beside the water

at moments like this I think of you
                                walking down to Acheron
your secrets crossing over   where the sign
beside the river reads *I flow with grief.*

A HISTORY OF SUNLIGHT

1

an orb spider hitches a strand to a branch
abacus of her viscera beading the movements

like me she's part of the rust and pulse
of the day falling and time only speaking
to the veiled face   to the whisperer
beneath the foliage   now wordless and still

speechless is one way for the weight
of the hibiscus to open   white against white
against light folding to half-light along the fence

speechless is one way for the traffic to run
down streets between the houses
pushing the inaccessible along a line of sight

cars pass with a sorrow shared between them
something lost when the motors were turned on
something like a promise to loneliness that was broken
loneliness of deep forests   old growths dark with genetic
drainage   everything that becomes lost
                              when it flows into presence

presence is what I saw yesterday in the dead robin
extending its wings on a slow glide into the earth
beetles moving like fingernails along its back
a scratch but no itch   head bowed into a cold climate
ground-flying to Netherworld   to other private trees.

2

the sky is shine corroding blue   clouds like seamounts
the neighbourhood softening to a fine dim silk
someone hitching it to a bough   someone weaving
the hours   one over the other   the highlights
and gloss braided along a hunger for infinity
and all that prettification cool against the skin

hours come and the gods keep busy in their corners
knitting chromosomes to disengagements   creating
pullouts of flesh and bone from apparitional dust
cut of the metaphysical   snip of the unknowable
signing everything in the low cuneiform of the self

sometimes the self peels away in late afternoon
moving off as the heat of the day collects on the faithful
on all those children playing madly in yards
all those flies with their snouts in the silk
those dogs running hard in their sleep
our lives wander off for a moment or an hour
and we never wish them back   it simply returns
simply enough like fetishes of absence
the shadowless idea of empty space
or the bodies of ghosts clinging
like damp newspapers to grass and to our wrists
as we reach for the car door   driving away
shredding numberless haunts of a physical world

I sit between the inner sides of my small landscape
by the roses   each a fortune-teller's table
a red fate   a white fate   stained by invocations
bees fly by with the strength of thumbs
crows fly by with the strength of hands
I sit unable to lift the hem of what surrounds me
Fate's diaphanous cloth of attitude and appearance
silks that breathe a transparence onto circumstance

I'm thinking of serenity's heartbeat carried on the breeze
just one beat   just once coming into what's to come

I think of Life pushing all of her heaven into spores
I think of Death walking behind us in the dark
his feet a swarm of hands picking up the distances
                                        lying on the floor.

3

the planet pedals on slowly in the heat
while chlorophyll moves it closer to the sun
while along the sidewalk pigeons carry no messages
other than the universe cooing to itself in supplication
down the block children rehearse being human
good practice   multiple repetitions of joy and ache
summer changelings   each boasting up their holding
each standing like a curtain about to be drawn

the solitude of children   this is the way of heaven
it's the same for adults   this feeling of otherness
like a body within our body   like someone else's
fingerprints having easy passage through our skin
someone disremembering the intrigue of our hands
so we drop the water glass and the fall is luminous

and those dark panes on the ground offering a view
reminding us of what rushes into light
expecting birth and a grace and a world to appear
the accident   the shattered moment   broken surfaces
all the small fractures in absence that brought us here

this is the way of heaven and I try not to forget
as two minuscule clouds drift by   almost motionless
carrying their single glass of water   afraid to spill it

this is the earth's signature   two clouds
and a damselfly gliding between them
till that almost imperceptible body fades on a mote
on a jot of the empyreal   little firmament   tuft of air

this is the way of heaven   that imperceptible fade
beating its wings to traverse the strategy of the self

the small self   that small silence lying to the night
                    saying it wakes when morning comes.

4

the afternoon slants into further hours   jays repeat
the grand speeches of the gods and the missing word
wounds in the pine tree vein a light into the underworld
of the little songs   roots singing blades of grass
through their sequences   singing us to otherness

a ball of flames over Cancer and Leo   a crab and a lion
then a dog barking in the street   vertical to reason
a dog's sweep of visual perception   dog-sized   dog-born
the second sight of animals counting the suns we never see

there's so little we comprehend   yet we keep coming back
to the world   to sit under a star equal to locality
equal to the light on our skin   to the warmth in our blood
each thought and deed a history of sunlight
while Fortune draws straws   who will live   who will die
whose ache will be the ache of poppies
whose will be the pain of towns on fire
day after day and some of our lives shepherded through
sleeping on nourishment   eating the lower food
while night comes in both sexes   mating the inner world
to the outer   otherness to otherness
while a breeze moves hieroglyphically   symbol by symbol
one for God   one for God's absence
while the given is a heartbeat and a half-demise
half-life of a visitation among the weeds
while attendance comes
while the rain comes handing out darkness
                                        like books to be read.

ALL OUR WONDER UNAVENGED

1

particles of evening warm themselves in the afternoon sun
pieces of solitude gather slowly   one under each ginkgo leaf

I sit on a rock of saddlebacked granite
                                        I sit in a world of abundance
a handful of bees goes down to the river   two handfuls return
you deadhead the dog rose and two stray curs appear

you deadhead a memory and two more appear
longer and deeper and more alive than the last

I remember my mother seated at the kitchen window
her cat's-eye glasses staring out into the night
trying to find divinity and divinity's reasons

my mother believed God moved the sparrows around day after day
as a teenager I believed the sparrows moved God around
all the inexhaustible crutches He leaned upon
all the underweights of silence to find His way

now the only god I believe in are the sparrows themselves
                                    unaltered by my belief
their wings contain hollow bones where a pantheon could pass through
and they do   hundreds pass through at every moment
this is how they fly   by allowing passage to earth's beliefs
the little deities of the big thunder and the rain that falls.

2

at my feet black ants run about   looking for a great storehouse
                    a little picnic   a little headhunting in the grass
they drink the dew and as far as I know curse nothing

I would like to curse nothing   to move about practicing quietism
perhaps find the great storehouse   do some headhunting
stick to a regime   the discipline of a feather falling
                                    from a sparrow's back
I would like to be called out and fall to the furthest limits of the finite
to a resting place among the relativity of all attributes
which would be home surely   where I began   where I no longer dwell
feeling time and space upon me now   a little dust in my eyes.

3

a few clouds move in   riding the intersections of ancient thought
across the sky   old ideas that floated upward   Confucian dialogues
Sumerian rumours   prayers to Pallas Athena   Persian satires
Druidical ethics   not gone   not absorbed   not forgotten   just there
influencing us still   carrying our lighter burdens and the clouds

from where I sit clouds cast shadows on the flowerbeds
perennials along the fence that bloom like glossy photographs
of themselves   bright flowers stripped from shining pages
from catalogues that never mention the plant that doesn't exist
the imagined yarrow that the mind owns
                        that has neither root nor stalk   leaf nor flower

all my thoughts are a divination with yarrow-sticks
and a mere filament of flame   a single mouse hair burning
deep in a canyon   lighting up less than an inch of dead embers
the big fire   the full consciousness having moved on immediately
travelling constantly   never resting while in nature
while under Heaven's luminous regard.

4

I've been seated here for three hours I think   difficult to be sure
without a watch or a column of diminishing sand
or a dog that scratches her head at ten minute intervals

time is a controversial work about which no one agrees
time's a bugger my grandmother said and she would know

time's a bugger and finitude a fluid state without a source

anyway time is passing for me and my piece of granite
no point thinking about it   separating it out
Cling to unity the Taoists said over and over
till the nettles repeated it generation to generation
till you hear it on the breeze sweeping across fields and ditches

I'd rather contemplate nettles   follow their leaves
back to Culpepper's herbal   to the tonics of Hildegard of Bingen
I'd rather make nettle tea and drink to Lao-Tzu
but a shadow glides by and I have to look up

a bald eagle flies over   making his way down to the river
to fish the afternoon away   calendrical wing beats
time's wordless doctrine upheld and maintained
the wounds of salmon like minutes cradled in the hour's arms.

5

late afternoon and the western sun-door still ajar
some hours to go before it closes   shadow hours
for the food gatherers to return to their mounds
for chickadees to follow their old ways
                              fables without end

cosmologies of shadows gather up the light
                         from under hostas and azaleas
many stories to be joined into one before night comes

only one story after the sun slips over the horizon
                              the one and the manifold
My face is the face of the Disk this is the deceased speaking from
The Egyptian Book of the Dead   from the other side of darkness
the bright side and its holy office trying to give us a hint
                              an initiation into eternity
so we might find the eternal in perceptual experience

so we might find our way in the world   and the oncoming twilight
is the perfect time to find our way   so the Celts believed
that sacred in-between time   between worlds   betwixt night and day
when all crossings are possible   freeing us from duality
Dharma Path the Buddhists call it
Pollen Path of Beauty to quote the wisdom of the Navaho
and the bees would agree returning once more from the banks of the river.

6

I sit on my rock watching dragonflies hover by
with their wings sheathed in calligraphy
listening to feral cats on the move
                    spreading their Tantric cries

while shadows grow taller and taller like adolescent boys

and dogs bark and dogs bark and I almost understand
their Indo-European tongues   their slang for sex   for death
their reasons for biting their masters   for venerating
the chase through the thickets   their unlimited awe
their wonder unavenged   all our wonder unavenged
all of it left hanging in the fetish-shine of the moment
a longing   a bit of animal-shine along our skin

they are nations the Koran says of the animals
and I believe it   a kinship of being and knowing
                              as deep as ours
as ancient as breath on the lips
and any meditation on this deepens our own being
humbles us before the cricket's leg and the badger's eye
and we should be humbled   fall to our knees

then comes stillness and listening

                             comes with kneeling
and listening is the language of the soil
                        Latin of the hawkweed
so I sit quietly without moving   while buried all around me
seeds lie on their sides   longing upwards to visible air
while dusk is falling   honeymooning the shadows
darkening the medicine   the metaphysics of the grass
while microbes repeat their silent mantras to themselves
soundless and drifting   all woebegone and woken
                all Buddhas of Immeasurable Light.

7

time to go indoors   drink from the glass
                                    eat from the plate
move the pages of a book around
or watch the news sway in its cradle of light

a few stars are up and Venus in her silks at the horizon
                                    fresh from the underworld
a tracery of myths hammered onto her body
passing our lives night after night
where we all sit at a dark gate waiting for it to open
dreaming of lifting the latch of Morning Star
and stepping through to redemption

redemption is a dark game someone once said and muffled
I would add   like the whisperer inside the fox
calling to the whisperer inside the varying hare
                                    a dark and distant game

too distant for me as I walk to the house

the moon is rising   cabbaging light from the weeds
full moon   full sides short of breath from the long climb

I walk and I could sleep in it   in the footsteps
in the motion given   jewel-give of the fireweed
scent-give of the lilies trying to keep all of summer down

I walk and birds are settling in for the evening
among the pine boughs   their small calls from tree to tree
like the voice of Proteus across his many forms.

CAMPFIRE

when I make a campfire the forest learns
of my poverty   my penury here on earth
the match flares and it's like going home
after trying to find your place in the world
and failing miserably

I sit waiting for night   it nears through
the verge   down on all fours
and familiar with no one but God

it comes slowly through the trees
like a black dog turning its head from side to side
like a seeing-eye dog without its owner
still showing blindness a way through the world.

A TRACE OF FINCHES

for Margo

standing on a hill overlooking the Minas Basin
the sea calm   hidebound with moonlight
stars and throwaway galaxies swaying east
Minerva's bird gliding west on his mouse-run

quiet up here among the colourless wands of spruce
moths tracing thin bracelets in the air
fireflies drifting about with their gnomish-milliwatts
hives sighing in the undergrowth   a streamlet
crawling to Byzantium   its eyes down in the moss

below farmhouses have nosed in for the night
a fire behind each dream   a solitude behind each fire

an angel should appear just about now   to still the stillness
a divine messenger to pat down the hair of the sleepers

instead there's this bit of faith floating out there
somewhere above the valley floor   a wild belief
that the earth will sustain us   see us through
that we'll be angeled through with light at the end

I like the comfort in that   the small gods in that
gods small as finches   I think of finches
because when those birds all rise together into the air
it's like all the holy places
                    pulling away at once from the earth

I like the comfort of finches   a song's redemption
a feather's nudge into flight at the appropriate moment

what better wings to carry the soul away
a trace of finches drifting up Mammon's outline
to be elegy-plated high across the grief of the world

a long grief finally at truce with our senses
a flutter of plumage and an avian resolve

the way opened to a lingering darkness
a wayward shine from the receding light
the way small birds arrive and take our breath away.

IN THE DREAM OF THE YELLOW BIRCHES

for Barry

> *Heaven is inscrutable,*
> *Earth keeps its secrets*
> —*Li Ho*

1

the sun's yellow throat at the horizon
the thunder keeping in touch
rain falling in choirs

I come inside to make tea and read
from *Poems of the Late T'ang*
to feel all those lost moments
resurrected in this afterlife
to feel the dead move slowly
like honey turning over in its comb.

2

pages slough off their words   remain blank
for a few moments when the cover is finally closed
when it opens out to a great distance

the reader also sheds what has been written
what remains is the light twice removed
from paper   essence of a weightless and thermal rise
                                 of blood
layering in where the words lost their way.

3

constellations rising above clouds and houses
sidereal enzymes drifting through the streets
one barking dog giving us a distraction from the zodiac
so add one more mutt to paradise   one more set of teeth
to bite down on perdition

also add this pseudoscorpion crawling across the wall
a minuscule piece of architecture from the *Book of Revelations*
now standing perfectly still   a perfect word in its chest
for its next move across the abyss.

4

the night four hours old   rain gone out to sea
God already sealing the lips of the sleepers with fire
angels already taking on the form of our ill effects
demi-present and yet bright in our dreams

hard to see the Mycenaean grave of each rose in the dark
each place where the colour of grace is buried
along with the first voice of the invisible

hard to see the inlay of ghosts in the spider's web
or sense the sleepers shining back from the other side
the sleep of others buoys up my hand and these hours
also this book-scorpion finally beginning its blush
                              and journey once again.

5

spider-optics checking me at the backdoor   black into black
the fingerboards of its legs spasm slightly in the silk
eight eyes on its face   two turned inward watching the silence
of the self   the self we share   shadow-crossed in the same
                                                    shadow

out there earwigs and cutworms filing down the begonias
a cat sleeping it off   the dead combing the yard's dark hair

a fine mist stretched out above the mulberry tree
holding its breath   living through its own disappearance
as we all do   fadeout to absolution on the far side of belief.

6

some breaks in the clouds revealing pieces of radiance
an extragalactic nebula or two above the mini-mall
a few autos-da-fé burning bright over cars of the heretics
soon the traffic will die   the earth will go still
stilled and brought to its weight on an azalea leaf

we live in a storyline on a spinning world   no escape
flash forward then back   flame up and out like a match
struck hard once against a wall   a pinch of fire
autobiographical fizzle   once and we go out.

7

when Heaven breathes out Hell breathes in
between breaths we write down the word *river*
                      and are carried along
we scribble the word *healing* on a wound
and place it in the current   but only once

tonight rebel yells   squealing tires
police sirens   ambulance sirens
all sailing by on a bottomless drop of water

tonight the celestial mandate is still upheld
so time shines forth from the undergrowth
so in the grass obscurity is indistinct from fame

later I will read what Solitude has written on
discarded boards   on the underside of stones
I will read the ten thousand chapters of the leaf's
                          fall to the earth.

8

the clouds are drifting west to east   prayer smoke
carrying our sorrows and lamentations far from the city
         two hundred chapters or so floating above us
unreadable and votive like the sky itself

up there it's still the third century BC   nothing has changed
the same doctrine looking back at us as the Taoists attended
the image of the imageless   unceasingly it continues

down here the backyard holds onto its medieval light
down here blood finds the rose   red finds its mate
and a feral destiny follows us through to the end.

9

bats glide by on the receding warmth of time
clouds brush away the clouds
more stars appear   stigmata bleeding infinity
                              into darkness

also a few nighthawks on pilgrimage   an owl
perched high on someone's afterlife   a housefly
dying a straw death   small spins and weak buzz
nerve endings unplugging
                       from night's diminished returns

a few rosebuds tonsured by aphids lean back
in their seats   a few skeletal weeds lean forward

such things that signed onto mortality
to an offer of weightlessness after the candles
are blown out   after the flames dampen down to ash

bone and flesh build the world in their own good sleep
build around a stillness always a lifetime away

we rise from the same place as the place itself
but half-lit by half-things shining off the guise

the moon has risen   the waxing part   sickle
in the lifeline   blood pouring out as darkness
all the way down to cars and 4x4s parked
and laid bare   waiting at the curb patiently
for the seen to be unseen
for the End Times and a long walk home.

10

July's bloodlines flow to an inner alchemy
apparitional and encrypted in our bodies
secret messages from old destinations
old silences of someone else's heart

dark hours feeding us from pursed lips
their tongues nudge ours and we swoon
like clouds touching pine trees   like
gardens moving out over water

we're given what will sustain us
a few fingerprints on the moonlight
one or two monks behind our backs
tending to quietude

some hieroglyphs afloat in the low places
filled with water   mosquito wings   bits of grass
hair   flakes of skin   which predicted our lives
our every word and gesture   every thought
preordained and written down in a hieratic form
of dross   outtakes of the fallen   fallen and
                                        undeciphered

we're summoned and held by what we never see
according to the teachings of the Masters
all our kingdoms lie skin deep on the ground
erased by our eyelids closing in prayer
or by any whisper from any promised land.

11

these night hours shapeless and moving
like tenderness along a sword's edge
before it is raised   like the passion
of the dog violet before it is seen

these hours waiting for us to cross over
to stumble in   trip over the martyrdom
of our first life and fall into our second
transformed and fearful   confluence
of semblance   bloodlines and ashes

frightening to accept it   dungeon-work
that inner life bound in darkness
                              by an intense grace

bound and held   small bead on a thin strand
carelessly hung between heaven and earth
somewhere out there above the milk vetch
above the fires twice born in the hive

not much security in that   not much camouflage
yet I find myself in God's sleep again and again
in the dream of the silver birches
                              taking root in the soil

yet I find myself witless and godless
constantly testing the air and water
for any little absolute anxious on our behalf

insecure and silent are the ways of the self
one life for another   one cloud for another
white chapters adrift   unreadable and votive

I try to follow Meister Eckhart's advice
Do exactly what you would do if you felt
most secure   sometimes it takes
sometimes it doesn't   meanwhile saints
graze on the begonias   meanwhile
ravens go to the edges of the earth
and return with our hearts in their beaks

the ones we thought were in our bodies
the ones we thought were redeemed.

FROM

BITE DOWN LITTLE WHISPER

2013

URSA IMMACULATE

night swept back over the headlands
someone's sign language alone in the forest
scratching words in the air   haunting
narrow spaces between the pines

hieroglyphical pheromones carried on the breeze
anagrammatical gestures almost apparitional
                                almost perceptible

midnight and a redtail asleep in his negative theology
luciferin shine of fireflies   a coyote folding the pleats
of her wound   swaying her god with the pain
with the suffering that falls through belief's chasm
that small caesura between flesh and bone

I've been sitting alone beside the lake   subbing
for a rock or a blade of grass   watching
the phrase *ex nihilo* feather the water's surface
and faces of the Julii shine out from drab houses
                                of the midge larvae

the moon puts on a clean white shirt and rises
I lean back into the blood of my shoulders
and neck   into the pure vowels of my spine
vocalic pins attaching vertebrae to nerves
what was mutely sung by everything nameless
                                    everything forgotten.

                    *

solitude is our nourishment and redemption
in a world that is sensed rather than understood
quietude our reprieve from the skin-trade
of language   so I come to seek refuge here
in the stillness spreading among evergreens
like the dissemination of algae   like nightjars flying
through first kisses and Chinese whispers

we should confine ourselves to the present
as Marcus Aurelius wrote   but it's a hard sell
when memories like pollen set ablaze
                    fall from the air
with their final wish for us in hand
reddening the meditative colours
of each moment   white and off-white
pearly counterpoint to words and meaning
moony phosphorescence in the marrow

moonlight makes the world seem more absent
the blood of things more secretive and present
phenomena hushed and all breathing space
lit by a saurian light   bioluminescent glow
in the brain stem   our reptilian brain
like a pre-existent prayer that sometimes
rises out of story and flesh

I stand up and walk along the water's edge
beside me a heron's footprints run line after line
like typographical errors in the glistening mud
above me moths chaperone the musculature
of stars and the Delphic shudder of a cloud
                prophesying a bright green world

it's difficult to know the sanctitude
of things   bloodsqualls metabolized
hatched and cross-hatched   blackened down
                        to flesh and gesture
hard to imagine all the tongues tied in the weeds
all the heartbeats time-lapsed beneath each stone
life incessantly singing to itself in the night
funereal lips and luminous throats

it's difficult to know the sanctitude
of ourselves   as we breathe the rapture of time's
cadences deep into our lungs   along with the given
sum and cipher of human concerns
downshifting them through vein and bone
our entire lives magnetized to a shining point
each day   able to be carried away with a sigh

in the end being human is a long and wordless
journey   ask the dead caught and released
along the margins of a stag's breath
ask them as they descend the wooden steps
of the birch trees   that go far underground
till they reach Ursa Major   Ursa Immaculate
                              Bear of the Clear Heart.

                    *

walking along the shore   every footstep
a homecoming   every blade of bracken
                    with a finger to its lips
the earth imagining a physical world
my body shoulder-deep in a Dantean fluidity
In the middle of my life, I went astray
and I awoke in a dark wood

in the middle of my life I'm standing
next to the quillwort   listening
to nettles grind their teeth   to saplings
asleep in their future branches
to my every thought like a breath
loosened from a windowpane

this is the hour when Ursa Major comes as
a supplication   stars like bees sworn to light
when all our religions feed the shadows
of uncertainty to its most silent angels
when all our philosophies sound like small
animals beating their children in the grass

this hour is called wearing dark clothes
beneath your skin   this is called walking
through the forest with zero gravity behind
your eyes   this is called sign language
without an owner   emptiness of this hour
this is called the pale jawline of infinity
and flesh   called opening your mouth
without a sound.

BARDO

first light of day inscribed on night's gravity
sweet breath of noumena between the pines
this is the path of the unconverted
                    the unwashed
its pentimento showing through
the blood   showing through grass and weeds
                    briar and brush

I made camp just beyond the pond
where algae live happily in the continuous
loop of their wedding nights
just south of where ravens are already flensing
bodies of the departed   and crickets live
with their glassine eyes   their lidless black paper
                    watching the world

all the night shinings go out like candles
two by two   certain eyes close while
others open   as a breeze braids through
the old growth of this hour   sun rising
ur-light giving the sense that everything
is in holy orders   that we all live
in the guise of ourselves   in a measure
            of space under a monk's cowl

pampered bacteria in the leaf mould
dead foxes in their vestments
the grasses' heart stretching on for miles
swamp water living the life of tea steeped
                              to intelligence

the cursive pulse of everything in synch
like a geothermal cipher   warm as a deer's core
and every footstep we take is just where
the world's edge dips into infinite space

this morning I walk carefully there   knowing
that the husks of dead flies and twigs dust
all the rooms of Paradise   that every windfall
apple has come to change the world.

this forest has the weight of a book at rest   one never written
never read   no plot or storyline   no author or cover   only two
fly-leaves and a spine   little green bird you fly away and return
fly away and return   they burn you   they cut you down
                                        and you return.

MAGNUM MYSTERIUM

I was the one who first placed a pair of eyes
in the darkness   I left them on a large black tree
on a rock face I left an ochre kiss
on each life the awful hush of carbon
on every sensation a perpetual sigh

at the pulse of every red movement in the body
I placed endless blue space to remind it
of death   I placed lungs in fish
and then changed my mind   I sang camarillas
and patted each organ into position around the sun

I was charismatic and circumboreal
a skitter of thoughts   a jangle of namesakes
I was a deep and dark intaglio at the end
of every nerve   a bailiwick at the far end
of every consciousness

I was wilderness   I made orphans out of ascension
I disposed of every elision except absence
and introduced piquerism to insects   flight to stones
I coddled magma and micro-organisms
I added digestion to every biome   a womb to every tooth

I placed God in the details and then said goodbye
I rode the thermals till I was solid   I walked the earth
till I was air   I surrendered only to dirt beneath my nails
to the hard pinch of sight in my head   to my own mystery
the hulking of my tongue   to dung in my hair

I subdued joy in the higher orders and let it grow
wild in the lower   I ran blood through
the stems of butterweed   fire through
the scapulae of rivers   I told the first nouns there
were no verbs   the language believed me
and the language fell down.

BIODIVERSITY IS THE MOTHER OF ALL BEAUTY

in memory of Judy Davis

when I think of blood drops and little hurts
entering a field   filling the field
when I think of dandelions off their leashes
and the Noh play of dragonflies   airborne
red and metallic blue   light as silk

when I think that one sigh was the progenitor
of all life   that the binding of oxygen
and hydrogen is the most erotic calligraphy
that every thought   human and otherwise
                    is an astronomical unit
that each is star-laced to its very core

when I think that inside every genome there
is a line of sight that surrounds the earth
that perception holds the evanescence
                of all things within itself
that atoms are in a perpetual state of bliss

when I think that deer move elegantly between
trees like the great tea master Rikyū
did among his bowls   that a deep-sea coral
off the Hawaiian Islands is 4000 years old

when I think of parallel universes colonizing
the edges of birdsong   when I think that
        synaesthesia is the language of God
that flesh covers a wider and deeper pilgrimage

when I sit here knowing this is a dying world
nothing could be more effortless   more sacred
than this sleepy forest at dawn.

IN THE WILDERNESS

death of language by a billion blades of grass
a billion cuts along every word   yet no reason
for regret   no reason to address the situation

night like mist coming off black jade   stars on their
red ride along the vein   wolves prowling the woods
with sunlight bright on the pads of their feet
white birches over all creation.

LINES WRITTEN BENEATH A STONE

like the Emperor Lo-Yang seeing a supernova
I watch the starved aster open its white flower
and know there's no going back to men.

BITE DOWN LITTLE WHISPER

1

the sky cradles an absent blood   silence of washed
veins through the trees   bloodlines flushed out
                                        and carried away

hematic glyphs written once in the air and erased

we are stained by the invisible in the lowering day
by the arterial blush of the world   meanwhile
the ghosts of our fallen hair rise up to heaven
our shed skin follows us through room after room

meanwhile our thin eyelids open and close
our home disappears   and reappears
as the sum of our vacant ontology

pale ache beneath our tongues   pale metaphysics

The land that is nowhere, that is our true home
I use these words as talismans
shining syllables to hang in the branches
for luck   for chimes when the wind returns.

2

late hours among the weeds   grass top-heavy
with exoskeletons   film noir and animal weights

cats beginning to head out across fields
dusk banked up against their fur like dark birds

a maggot with a gondola's long shine over water
skimming the surface of a mouse lying in the brome

a doe standing still in the acquittal of light
each leg holding a presolar energy
                    and a mouthful of air

and we're there most days as witnesses
pressing our headaches against windowpanes
watching and waiting for time to gather us in
waiting for strange brushstrokes across our hearts
our hands just out of reach   our sight laid low
                                    in the guise

death filling in the blanks as holy writ and a steady grace
nothing profane   micro-organisms written
as sacred text on the painted tissue of things as they curl
as they die and are assimilated   curl and fall.

3

the end of day is a tapestry of one thread
laid flat across the landscape   a thin string
pulling sparrows up and over black hills

evening comes   dharma of bruised lips
blowing out the candles   loosening light
and time around the heart

so that night is a brief hurt among the illuminations
and sleep is an anatomy lesson without a body.

4

midnight or thereabouts   clouds gathering
like pressed flowers in a weightless book

a few stars on black paper   a few missing

among pine trees I've built a small life
a temporary narrative   ogham cuts in solitude
my fire swaying   deepening nature's blush
night's drift carrying that shine away

a night with a bad tooth in its jaw
the ache snug between ferns
a whisper of pain   telegenic among
hawk's beard and groundsel
among intercessions of the vetchling

there is no metaphor for such inflictions
so bite down little whisper   black incisor
right there where the inaccessible meets stillness
where yesterday's words draw the light in

bite down and sit tight   just there
where my fingers look for solitude
in the landscape   along mossy
stitches in the wood   along jinx
and orifice   dung and honey
where our shudders first ruptured
                        into language

language into deeper sleep.

5

camo of deep woods   black and grey
double dyed on quietude   tincted
with shadows of coyotes blading by
eviscerators flat against the breeze

hunter and hunted bloodied   processional
Vedic lip-synch of teeth on flesh
If the slayer thinks that he slays, and the slain
thinks that he is slain, neither knows the
ways of truth

so bite down little whisper   right there
where we live layered between form
                        and formlessness

where words from the Upanishads
are like bedclothes laid on the living
and the dead ... *neither knows*
the ways of truth   I kneel to this
every time   without knowing why

on nights like this it gives me comfort

on nights when I would rather
be a rabbit orbiting a celestial hunger
lost in the clover's gravitational pull
or one of those crows high in the branches
above me   just out of God's reach
splinters of sleep passing through their bodies
each feather trembling in its separate dream
each shiver holding twelve skies.

6

I tend my fire   a little lip at flame's end
a little curl of speech turned to smoke and ash
something redemptive in the burning wood
almost spoken of in the moment   almost heard

moon rising   white cathedral where we all
eventually go to pray   our only church
when we try to hush the dog and hush the rose
listening for improvisations of the one silence
one emptiness   ear to stone

I tend my fire   a little galaxy at flame's end
a little curl of sidereal time turned to smoke and ash
burning dry sticks and branches   a reclusive
iconography   melancholia and its sacrament
                              drear and aura

drowse of the absolute somewhere above me
cloistered and nodding off among microbes
among changelings and starvelings
incessantly drifting   little fadeaways
on their deep journeys through the virga

seated beneath the overhang of pine boughs
my grief and ignorance want for nothing
feed off an absence   autolytic and bittersweet
feed off a synaptic loss   that space between
two words   where our souls will finally
            be tonsured and nail-clipped
our hearts sewn shut over our eyes

tonight I bow my head   tonight the darkness
bows back at me from its shining abyss

meanwhile a chrysalis retools its enzymes

meanwhile grasses grow along the deer path
each a copy of a beautiful mother.

UNBORN

Charon folding water   Morpheus folding dreams
a dark road ahead of us   a dark forest with whispers
where the leaves should be   not clouds overhead
but an afterlife   not wind but a laying on of hands

evening came down from the mountain to reassure us
with its presence   its footprints without footsteps
sight without eyes   it held us and we felt like grass
moving through grass   like a sigh along a riverbed

we stood in each other's shadow   lay in each other's arms
vertebrates   invertebrates   every possible form
and like numina we drew sleep from stones   breath from fire
like virga we sang of a reality deeper than the mind.

1

early hours   moon hidden in the wings   the dead in their small
apartments   bent heavily over paperwork till dawn   little night things
set adrift   feral cries   sleep-driven just beyond sleep

I'm waiting for the preordained visitant to appear   the aphasic breath
that licks the soul clean   shadow's understudy   eternity's beautiful dog
that comes to wash the humanity from our blood

                                    just for a moment or two

in the hope that we can see the further reaches of our being
the going to and coming back   enriched by our journey   by journey's
end among arteries of lost voices in the flesh.

2

whatever has been thought or felt was first written down
before the Holocene   beneath pigment applied to a rock face
yellow ochre in the shape of a horse
or an ibex   still we putter about thinking ourselves new
only human of course   only animal   our phrasal teeth gnawing
on windfallen bones from someone else's
idiom   still we're happy enough on the good days
                                                bleeding out on the bad

burnishing our words   we hold them up   expecting miracles
                      radiance at the darkest moment of the night
without realizing each night enters holy orders long before sunrise
martyrdom and fade-out   a cowl's melancholia
pulled down quietly over the hours   all the sin-eaters in synch
before day breaks   before we begin our sequence of supplications
little prayers for the long commute
to a near-truth   for all the goodbyes between names and destinations.

3

our sense of loss is visceral   a fine tuning of dross in the body
a sharp sting felt on the other side of perception
like silhouettes calving in the taiga
                            just beyond our consciousness

all those shadows that will one day be stitched into our skin
refolded   slid into our veins

all the while longing for our wounds to be removed   pocketed in red
linen and carried away   to be stealthily hidden
                            behind a cat's hair or a grain of sand

longing for an incorruptible redemption to carry us forth
in a raven's beak   in a rabbit's foot
bearing us through evergreens in a slow waltz and glide
to that place between our eyes   where the soul first muddled
into a physical world   first experienced thought
its apparitional flow and pulse   its low burn into our tissues
its fire and stake   its postpartum auto-da-fé.

4

there are deer asleep in the hills   their slow breathing
                    lifting up the tell of a thing lost
something with lamentations on its back
something made of belief and unbelief in equal measure

there are also angels sending messages from stone to stone
with mezzo heartbeats but no chain of command   no controller
                    no Lord of Illuminations and Afflictions

we exist between deer and angels   between earth and earth's
reflection   we originate out of the soughing and reshuffling
of wind and cloud   cloud and blood

tonight the clouds circumnavigate a sprig of bitterweed
broken   lying on the ground   all of its rooms darkened now
all its doors unlatched   we stand on its roof to watch
the stars   enthralled   mum   caught up in eternity

and they look back at us   like God we want to say   but don't.

5

under the child-rearing stars   beneath the welkin petalled with black
flames
there are times when the self is inconceivable
when whatever was made of mind and body is unmade   laid to rest
a bit of grey ash on a scry's prophetic thermal

here deep in the forest   in the stillness of ecocide
in the quietude between spruce trees   when absence redeems you
when the world is rising and leaving
                                    when you've forgotten your name
forgotten the wistful knot of air that is your spirit
that's when the ancients say you'll reach the bottom of things
and start upwards again   on the bodings of an ascent
beyond the grief of your infirmities   that's good medicine
the ache of return outside the self
the winged offspring of your cells pressing flight
a dark drop of genesis for the soul's shudder and climb.

UNCOLLECTED

2014–2021

FIELD NOTES

we are raised among lupines and atrocities
among insects and their lamentations
where there are no gods left in the clouds
no darkness apart from darkness

meanwhile rocks click their claws
and evergreens tap down below the storyline

meanwhile someone's voice-over wears thin
on its long journey across the lake   lisp among
duckweed   whimper among the reeds.

*

we're all slaves to something   for me it's
that whitetail standing motionless on the shore
saint of the held breath   saint of the afterimage
and just behind him the unborn   resettled
tucked in beneath dogwoods   with their milk
teeth jewelling down their spines
hearing only the atonal gossip
                    of the untranslatable
sighs and cries from the edges of things.

                *

once in a while our wishes come true
and we fall into place beside a pebble
on its long roll across the ocean floor
that sacred stone of sweet oblivion
which we never see coming   little black thing
round on the top   round on the bottom

once in a great while we put our flesh aside
fold it like red linen and lay it on meadow grass
and then we drift along towards a new life
like a grosbeak does   a last breath and a long flight.

*

river of moonlight   mosquito teeth
frog song   foxes running up and down
the hill   the weight of their footsteps
like jade buttons on an empty sleeve

sweep and slide of night through the trees
all the waters moving west   all my thoughts
east of me now   bodying darkness in the hollows

I wonder what prehensile psalm waits
among the roots tonight
                    when I lie down my head
what will hold me in my rabbit-sleep.

BESTIARY OF THE RAINDROP

1 *Genesis*

it begins here I think   with a raindrop
with a raindrop and a world   with a cloud
and the cool morning air interlaced
with hot breath from under stones

it begins each morning with a few cloudlings
drifting toward the horizon
                    the horizon drifting toward
the vast spaces between elementary particles

it originates with a landscape written quietly
with its haemophiliac punctuation and storyline
with conifers and hardwoods   wet soil and rootage
while below ground the darkness is almost flesh
almost manifest   the arisen drifting between trees
each one the colour of a proverb   colour of rain
each with a life pushed into its body   twisted in
                    twice   first left and then right.

2 Otherkin

all night people slept under a milkfed moon
their hopes like threadpulls on a sleeve
their dreams rinsed in the mind's secondary light
each breath in time-lapse   each heartbeat lifting
its own deep weight from out of the past

when they woke the resplendence of what's
indefinable carried them forth   one enthrallment
at a time   they were greeted by a sunshower
and a sky the colour you might find on a postcard
from Alsace or on the surface of Ganymede
a mizzle and a few putti rabbiting on   up in their high
corners   a bit of a breeze over the penciling of veins
in new flesh   over each heart held by red leashes
to the body   over combings of sunlight through the weeds
axis mundi in every flower   a dog-throated syntax
from beyond those hills   the brome holding tight to the soil
the blades of grass clicking into place one by one
like latches as the sun rises   they hold something deep
beneath the soil that's precious   a knowledge
so cherished they never speak of it   even to each other

they know that what falls to the earth could become a wolf
or a snail   or a man jacklighted by stars
they know all rain is made of shapeshifters   changelings
and otherkin   that God is a raindrop   nothing more.

3 *Empty Reliquaries*

morning of the gone-away   with its Easter weeds
slipware sky   morning lifted up by its four corners
and shaken twice to bring the rain   a mossed gravity
between the trees   holding the not-yet or the might-be

quick destinations and a bit of nevermind
move the ravens through the air   from tree to tree
                                from wound to wound
each beat of their wings a retelling of sunlight sliding
between feathers eons ago   one narrative
keeps them airborne   one story darkening in flight
archaeology of the ants digging down toward
their own memories of the earth   soil a mega-narrative
and paradigm shift   the darkness there almost silent
                                as we are almost dust

as we are the destiny of dust   one destiny among many
each life risen out of ur-ground   along with our nostalgia
for primordial wholeness   for the borders of paradise
so heaven's after-hours can be worn next to our skin
holding flesh to bone   raindrop to ocean.

                    *

clouds at a standstill   finches flecked with gold
sutures opening on a dead beetle's back   beside it
someone's silence travelling close to the ground
to continue its journey across the next inch of reality
then onto the ends of the earth

dull ache of oxygen   braiding of sky and evergreens
windfall light in the grass   all the lines and crevices
in the rocks where memories can seep through to oblivion
memories sounding like water sliding down marble stairs
the blue bicycle   the weeping doll   the first touch
like rain-water spreading across marble till they disappear.

                    *

a late spring   the season pretty much prepartum still
little happening aside from some interwork
at the soil's edge   each new grass blade holding
onto its measure of light   buds on the maples
                    along this narrow dirt road

no plot or counterplot here   just a little urge and cry
somewhere between the trees   a squall along
the edges of the map   something dying or being born
grading in or out of a given world

these back roads lead nowhere   winding through dried
yarrow stalks and rotting pine needles   through bare
bones and spare parts   realm of amnesia's angel
                    kingdom of empty reliquaries
the dead matrixing   seeing bodies and faces
of the living in the fallen leaves.

4 *Cloud Walking*

wet morning   a mind phrasing within each drop of rain
rapture's silver on the branches of pine trees
                    blank page of the lake awaiting its scribe

a one inch breeze moving two or three blades of grass
like the sweet breath of a cricket blowing in
                        from the other side

this day was begotten far back   when granite and blood
first received their sight   this day was born peregrine
a wanderer   its legs like long farewells

this day is a cloud-walker   clouds as white as Saint Philomena's
sleeves   floating and weightless   remembering their way
                    along the grey shell of morning

clouds bookmark the spirit   show us what passage
to return to   show us where the text is channelling
in the Light and its protocols   clouds populate
the earth   bear clouds   human clouds
dolphin clouds   so much vapour and mist
so many bodies to carry the rain around
all of us living in the bestiary of the raindrop.

                    *

I travel where only clouds could lead me   this is the path
I take to get nowhere   this is the path bare-backed
and ridden by stars all night   this is the path swanning off
into chthonic light   somewhere beyond the edge of things

cloud watching whets the heart   beneath its weight
the divine finds form   a brushwork of foxes on a ridge
a rabbit nibbling at the roots of paradise   a man curled
up on a cockle shell   goldfinches stitching the air behind
                                                        them as they fly

also a cinch of sparrows overhead   Manichaean shadows
along the grass   a duality of one   or one and a bit
the half-life of our pleasures like wood smoke in the trees
our infirmities drawing in the light of feral things
eventually all light becomes Purgatory light
and it overspreads   all things become transubstantiated
and unbidden   including us with our tongues
                                        between our teeth
with our trespasses monotonous   unvarying in pitch
nothing much in the end   just a scratch in silverpoint
                                        sinnings with beetle-shine
and grub-crawl   inchlings across sad terrain

it doesn't matter where you come from or who
you've been   we're all heading for the same place
beneath that flat rock lying out in the meadow
not a gravestone but a timepiece
time's stone knife skinning down each hour
a rock under which there are spaces like chambers
of the heart   filled with a great distance
and a votive silence
            containing optograms and fugues
red offerings and bones prinking flesh from memory.

                    *

a million bodhisattvas in the circumference of a nod
a million nobodies just like you and I   our fretting
keeping the rain company   splendid in its
pre-Columbian glow on the poplar leaves

wandering through the forest   no one around
a green gloss on everything and the drizzle putting
in its time   while we walk we are our own salvation
while we sleep we say grace with our wounds
while time is the next word out of our mouths
longing for breath and other unknowable things

time granulates martyrdoms in the tall grass
the broken katydid   the half-eaten salamander
the gadding moth on its back   kicking at the air
these are the saints I trust   the measure of a god
made wholly of aftermaths and inclement graces

this is the god of the imago   its metamorphosis
and song   its savage prayer and second skin
this is the god of the wolf   with its slit heart
and wild conceits   this is the god of the shadow
life   its bright hands in bright water.

*

small passages of light through the trees
voices in the deadfall   skin and gristle
in the underlife   an angel to write
              in the margins of our thoughts
a jinn to flashlight our eyes in the dark

I want to see what the dead see in the shining
light of day   what the darkness sees written beneath
our nails   I want to go to all the outposts of bone
and flesh   just to listen to the geographies
of eye and tongue   I want to sit in a meadow
with nothing to hold me to the earth
like a tier without a knot   I want the Devil to play
the white keys while I play the black   I want
my spirit to listen and say nothing   not a word

the spirit gathers no dust but not so the solitude of the spirit
not so the weight of pines and clouds upon the spirit
nor the outtakes   a hush and a still life   each raindrop
a millimetre or so of mercy just above the forest
a drop of water leaving the sky for the earth   eventually
leaving the earth for the sky and returning again
what an immeasurable journey over billions of years
The mind moves with the ten thousand things as Manura said
and just now my mind moves with the rain   it falls and rises
and falls again   there is no self in all this movement
there is no end to this beginning.

BIRTHDAY

there was just enough evening left for me   just enough grayscale left
to move into the blackness   to wait there as many travellers had before
to wait for the tracings of birthplaces beyond the fittings of language
and intent   places to be born and reborn   names to be unborn
in the rhizomorphic soil   identities to evaporate through transpiration
              along the bending backs of ferns

on the night I was born my thoughts were origamic foldings of dark law
my beliefs had blood whispered into them   one by one   drop by drop
my eyes crackled like attended fires   my tongue woke to the accumulated
wisdom of hillsides and ideological shifts in the river's current
on the night I was born my hands chose the penmanship of cicadas
              my feet selected the speed of newts

on the night I was born there was a wide scattering of gravity and trees
there was the veering grace of bats and the vanities of diatoms
clouds billowed offshore   phosphorescent plankton shone like heavenly
hosts and my skin had an odd warmth to it   like the caressive fluidity
of evolutionary ancestors coming up through the flesh   like the nearer
gods of time and space shining brightly through the otherhood
              of stars and pinpricks of orbiting light.

A THIN PLACE

1

summer solace   the gods give way and the day is
unsealed   affinities fall into place   the morning air
fills with a jink of sparrows
                    and the co-consciousness of bees

a bit of rain is falling   like eyedrops   one by one
with hardly a cloud in the sky
grass blades look like papercuts
        each red from the slant light of the rising sun.

*

rain is a divine presence no matter how you approach it
regardless of your angle of intent   rain with its ear
to the ground hears the held pulse of the soil
hears the hardpan's sigh inspirited with a plurality
of messages for all the spiders this side of Elysium
all the fish hushed up in waves   wolves and coyotes
for curlews loitering overhead   for the black river under
the earth   whose waters nurture us to the very end

every place the rain falls becomes a *thin place* for a time
where you can cross over to the other side
                    and read its colourless calligraphy—
all the names of transcendence   all the placeholders
of being   all the hamartias of thought and flesh
before they are realized   all the accompanying shadows
waiting   pigmented just beyond our desires.

                    *

early morning is a braiding of breath and breathlessness
                    a confirmation and negation of wounds
an austere silence   an unhearable absence that passes
                    over us unseen   like a dark forest
                    scarcely a centimetre or so above our heads
this is what night left behind   what our lives leave behind
when we're gone   that and our dead bodies standing
like seamarks on the broad waters between this world
and the next   between this heartbeat and the one
that never arrives   that stays perched on a small branch
perfectly still   just out of the wind.

2

a sunshower   light and unscrolling   freckling grass
            and all the engendering beasts
all those blood-carrying memories of the Cenozoic
all the wildlings who will inherit the earth once again
as we consume our own lights   ingest our ashes
                    and move into the outer darkness.

                *

the earthy scent of petrichor   that smell of spacetime
across the landscape   the day heartfelt and bereft
of meaning   fledge of sunlight   feathery fire on spruce
boughs   on an inscription of ants along the ground
moveable type   that spells out something about what
lies unkissed and laid down in the dust   what is unborn
again   what is unremembered
                    shadow-gripped and laid down.

                *

on the altars of the world we have placed our libations
and fetishes   we have lit our candles and incense
from time zone to time zone we have carried our prayers
on our backs   we have endured the luminous lethargies
of various gods   we have called out to mathematics for help
            searched for unobtainium in the vastness of space
and looked directly into the sun till we went blind

but all the time something unknowable was bending
the meadow grasses ever so slightly and we longed
for its gaze   for its footstep and whisper deep
in the piney wood   in the green distances of a planet
hidden between stars   a planet that is a fetishization
of water and stone   a world that's a soft light and a slow
sleep   a world like an apparitional bee flying through
a hive   little ghost   little curtain call.

3

the wind picks up   pinions backpedal along a crow's wing
while mosquitoes diagram the air beneath a grove of alders
where the quiet is an eavesdrop and a round edge
where each thought is an awayness   that moves deeply
                    into the dimensionality of the moment

there are no orisons here   no beatific prayer to the firmament
or even a wind-borne sigh   only a single heartbeat
in suspension   like a breath held in amber   its dark edges
collapsing in on itself   waiting to push blood through a body
                    no longer standing there
last vestiges of its flesh outsourced and theoretical now.

                    *

landscape is a stand-in for the mind   a stand-in for memory
for the remembered trees of childhood   each frescoed
on a neuron   each like a lightning flower on the chest
landscape and mind   simple joys orbiting the sun in equal
measure   dark places and bright places   both in equal measure
uncomplicated really   simple as a flash of light in an insect's
fibrous eye or a small feather resting on the back of your hand
                    breathe too heavily and it floats away

the mind is the afterlife of nothingness   the imagined world
with its imagined gestures   the mind is a bit like a mosquito
a bit like an alder grove   like a braiding of breath
                                        and breathlessness
the mind is the place where the sun slips inside to warm itself
where the moon keeps its white books   the ones no one reads
each book a grimoire   each page a fork in the road
each destination a hiding place   a curled leaf   a rusty pail
the cartography of lichen   old doors in the sky.

NOCTURNE

1

I have my night   my hours of greater magnitude
my time to settle in with the essential form of things

I have fireflies and catchlights moving between the trees
a deer's porcelain footprints along the ground   a vapour
of rabbits in the hills   I have the pulse of stones
and the dead ribboning through
                              the uncombed grass

each night I lay down with the ghosts of pikaia
and become glamoured by their incandescence
their glow like that last sunset in Doggerland
like the shimmer of DNA sequences ancestrally
inserted into a genome   that bounty of light
              in the germline.

2

a quiet night   clouds rolling in   the microgravity
of a single thought somewhere out there in the dark
it might be one of my own   it might be something
created in the Palaeolithic   still wandering about
                  like the exoskeletal remains
of insects adrift in the air   or simply be the spindrift
of comprehension between one life and another

I'm walking down to the lake   with a dappling
of moonlight across the forest floor
with stars overhead migrating like fetal cells
                        into their mother's body
a lip of water around a stone quivers
flies among the bitterweed polish their lenses
while angels in their ghillie-suits
shift their positions
                  under the cover of darkness

out here human realities don't matter much
and yet this is where you'll find transcendence
the soul-enveloping absence that is the inner life
this is where you'll find the true weight
                              of consciousness
those emanations of cloudless time
cerulean blue   threading thought to flesh
flesh to intuition   preordained like a fine
dust to fall on the loved and the unloved
              in equal measure.

3

there's an old Arab saying
               night is the poet's day
I like that and night's dharma   black-gripped
around each tree and blade of grass
               holding tough to the tenderest gesture
to all the metamorphoses of a singularity

I like my unceasing belief that I exist   the way
I turn my head when my name is called
the way night questions all my assumptions
as I walk   as I add my shadow to other shadows
               to the dark deities of post-belief
as I listen to someone shelling crickets
as I listen to the hymns of ditch water and cattails
mother-water carrying intercellular activity
at the intersection of corona and birth

I am one of those always in a liminal state
               always thinning into reality
then fading out again   always following
those lost on that journey
between one thought and another.

4

I walk along depending upon the surface of things
                    and loose approximations of thought
I have small reasons for what I do
for the blending of cognition and deed
I rely on the stabilizing properties of whisperings
                        exquisite and venerable
murmurations in the undergrowth   leaf-talk
and moss-chant   all that chlorophyll has to offer

my footsteps contain all the hard labour
                of petals falling on lace
I move quietly   slowly   a walking
meditation   a sleepwalker with no bed
to return to   walking down an old logging
road   overgrown with goatweed and fleabane
              I am the sleeping one
I long for the mediumship of cicadas
the foretelling of their seventeen-year voice
the sweet arcane of their chorus to guide me

I look for the mercy of lost places   for a place
that's not a place at all   I look for precious things
transformations of allegiances and pain
as I pass swamps and cranberry bogs
I look for the lowest places   ones that might
teach me how to breathe like earth and water
help me find a place
                 time-lapsed between heartbeats

after walking for hours   standing beside
the lake   beneath a convergence of planets
surrounded by the synchronicity of being
each tree in a gravity well   each rock
cradling the radius of a supplication
I have gained and lost my worldly senses
I have become the very lack of me
                 I have become the luminous sleep
under all this darkness   I am the sleeping one
                 I age into dreams.

THE GONENESS OF LOST THINGS

for Autumn

we wake from sleep with all our dreams
forming a glory around our head
we wake with a transfusion of moonlight
  just beneath our skin
with all our thoughts steepled in light

our dreams like grace notes on still water
like bees singing honey into a hive
yet our days are weatherworn a beetling
across the hours each life a slow spin
 of quanta on the head of a pin
with a planck length of wisdom
   to see us through to the end

we wake to a bandaging of sunlight
across a field to a bit of divination
braided overnight into the trees
we wake to the intentionality
of interacting particles to a place
where sighing is an alchemical art
where evensong is landfall

we step out into a bright world
to be greeted by the century's shift
towards a discernible shape
by the weight of the sea's blue tongue
        resting against the shore
to a world where every moment is a lost
memory   the goneness of lost things

we are what our dreams have made of us
ours is a reality lived in cognitive intervals
        between joy and melancholy
our lives unanswerable to the *is-ness*
of things   all of our time lost to locational
drift   heading towards the waiting darkness
all our words like glacial striations
                    in our collective memory
language talismanically present
                    in our connective tissue
meanings like blood waxing and waning
in a vein   all of this on a small blue planet
all of this beneath dying stars

our dreams wait for us to take our
rightful place beside a tree or a stone
to stand knowing the cells of our body are
distant messages gathered across vast
                              stretches of time
that our thoughts are threadlets of shadow
seeking passage through the weeds
that each of us is sanctified
                              by carrying a blade
of grass or a drop of rain against our heart
by carrying a bit of fire from the Neolithic
deep in our bones   enshrining that flame
ensouling the light   bowing our head
to where all the mothers are sleeping.

A PRAYER OF THANKS

for the marriage of woodland
and moonlight   for the intergalactic
breath that carries wonder between
worlds   for the cumulus cloud
for the bride of newly fallen snow.

POETRY AND THE SACRED

A Ralph Gustafson lecture

My talk this evening is about poetry and the sacred. It's a theme I've kept going back to for over thirty years now. For me, there's an intimate connection between the two, so intimate in fact that I can't really separate them out, one from the other. It's been the reason why I have continued to write; otherwise, I don't honestly think I would.

There's an umbilical point somewhere that nurtures both, like twins fed from the same source. By *sacred*, I don't necessarily mean religious, or spiritual in the New Age sense of that word. I mean the fundamental experience one has with time and space, with the seemingly endless corporeality that flows into our consciousness. I mean how each thing holds a mystery, simply because it exists, because existence itself is sacred. The fact that something exists at all has continued to amaze me, and the forms, as well, have amazed me. I don't mean this in a sentimental way; true amazement asks far more from us than the recognition of beauty and form. Amazement also demands that we see the darkness inherent in everything, that we see the destructiveness implicit in creation and its attending grief. Poetry helps to enhance and deepen our experience of existence, not just by the use of words, but by the fact that despite their use something else is carried along with them.

At the heart of poetry is a pre-verbal reality, a calling forth from a core within our being. There is something in poetry that pushes us beyond language. It's as if the language used negated itself and opened up well beyond linguistic meaning, into a realm that has far more to do with communion than communication. Poetry derives its energies and interests, to a great degree, from an extralinguistic view of itself and its meaning. It transcends what is written on the page. Poetry carries us, not just on the backs of words, but also on the spaces between the words.

This is why some teachers have a difficult time teaching poetry; they are always looking for meaning, while sometimes driving their students to distraction with the search. It becomes a game of *Where's Waldo*, but poor old Waldo isn't there. There is no objective meaning. Meaning is what you bring to the poem, not just what the poet has written. Meaning is very arbitrary. In the end, the poem is the integrity of a moment lost in the enormity of that moment and found again on the far side of any linear meaning. The words themselves point to where no words can go, where the textual intent becomes secondary to where the poem is directing us.

As Buddhists say, you shouldn't confuse the finger pointing at the moon for the moon itself. In other words, you shouldn't think that believing in the teachings of the Buddha means you're a Buddhist, but rather you should look to where the teachings are pointing. Believe in the moon, not the finger. Poets, the politics of poetry, the prizes, etcetera, are meaningless in the face of the moon itself. Often, the moonlight is lost and we forget why the poems are there, why we're standing outside, looking up at the night sky.

The poem, as Archibald Macleish said, shouldn't *mean* but *be*. Creating being is the Great Mystery re-enacted on the page and in the psyche. Once it was considered stealing fire from the gods; in our society, it's keeping a sacred fire alive amid the destructiveness and greed that is an ever-present darkness we must navigate daily. Donald Hall once said that poetry in this culture is a revolutionary act. Not just the writing of it but the reading of poetry as well, an act of rebellion in a world so bent on hiding the experience of the sacred.

Mindfulness, one of the main components of poetry, has become a subversive act in a civilization so fixated on the self. It's a sad commentary on our society when opening up our hearts and eyes has become seditious behaviour. Without mindfulness, there is no poetry, no art, no spiritual development, only the barrenness of a self separated from the rest of existence.

It takes a great deal of effort to see what's in front of you, whether that's a stone, a mountain, or another person. After much watching, after much witnessing of the metamorphoses from object to presence, you find that everything is self-luminous. If you observe something long enough, its being comes forth, the *isness* of the thing is made manifest. You end up feeling the sacredness of its presence in time and space. In *Ulysses*, James Joyce says it well: "Any object, intensely regarded, may be a gate of access to the incorruptible eon of the gods." What you're experiencing is the being of what has been attended by your sight and patience. What you're feeling is a connective pulse, the conjunction of seer and seen, the prime ritual of the sacred. This is what the great Dominican mystic Meister

Eckhart meant when he said, "The eye with which I see God is the same eye with which God sees me." The watcher and the watched are one and the same, as the poet and the reader are one when their spiritual centre of gravity has been altered by the poem. The poem can allow us a perspective beyond the culture and iconography used to create it. The poem has no culture or language to steadfastly support its framework; it is more an act of nature, operating outside the constructs of a given society.

Art, in the end, will save us from "culture," from the rigid notions we have of the world and our place in it. The forgotten dimensions of our lives are given back to us; we are returned to our deeper selves, shown again our interconnectedness with the universe at large. That nuclear moment can happen while viewing a painting, reading a poem, listening to a piece of music, etcetera. It can also happen while seated on a hill overlooking a landscape, or staring into the night sky, or simply watching someone drink a cup of tea. All you need is mindfulness, openness to the moment offered. Poetry comes from these moments, from the longing to reanimate them, to give them new life and energy, to capture at least some of the wonder they contain. They come from our desire to cross over, to connect and interact with a larger view of reality, to break out of the confines of our small definition of the self, that claustrophobic fear of leaving the comfortable routines that define us. To these moments, language is an impediment, the weight of cliché, common usage, etcetera, pressing down heavily on each line written.

Metaphor is one way to re-establish our relationship with the textual possibilities; it sidesteps many of the pitfalls that lock language in a low, weak orbit around the individual. If the cliché that poetry allows us to see with fresh eyes is true, metaphor, to paraphrase Eckhart, is the eye that both the world and the poet use to see each other. It creates sight where there was none; it releases us to new expectations. Reality shifts and we are carried along with the movement. "Metaphor," to quote Cynthia Ozick, "is the mind's opposable thumb." It allows us to grasp meaning in one of the mind's darkest places, in that gap between the meanings themselves, in that fissure created by polarities, where light falls to blackness. To find the connection between dissimilar things is to place a flame there. In that deep chasm lies the consecrated space, the sacred ground of all spiritual traditions. The poet can bring back to our modern consciousness much of what has been lost during our journey towards mechanized existence. From the pilgrimages poets make, we are reminded of the heart's great need for wonder, its longing for a transpersonal dimension in our lives. Inside each of us is a desire for expansion outside of our ordinary self, to extend our understanding of nature, the universe and other people. Poetry is one way that this can be realized.

Our brains have evolved to exist and navigate in a narrow range of reality. For example, we see things as solid, when in fact they consist mostly of empty space. Few of us are aware that we are living on a planet travelling at 105 000 kilometres per hour through the vastness of space, and that our galaxy, the Milky Way, travels at 210 kilometres per second. We see only a small part of the electromagnetic spectrum; we live within the scale and orders of magnitude that present themselves to us. We judge all of this as normal and often pride ourselves on being realists. The truth is, like any other creature, we have strict limitations on what we can perceive.

Likewise, language itself seems real, something we can depend upon. We think with it, we communicate with it, we use it to have imaginary conversations with people, even with people who are dead. We rely on the solidness of words, but like objects, they are made up mostly of empty space. They don't define, they indicate, they suggest reality. Language and reality are always in a state of becoming. Neither reaches formation, neither is ever totally realized. Actuality is always elsewhere. We move towards it, but it keeps well ahead of us. What we have as human beings are possible moments of a larger dimension. Most of us trust only to our five senses, the five reasons that hold us to a view of the self as something distinct from the rest of existence. Poetry tries to reach out and connect with more than our senses allow, attempting to discover what lies beyond the confines of our narrow perspective.

Poetry asks that we reshape ourselves, and in that reshaping discover the sacredness of what surrounds us. It lies everywhere and in everything. Christ says in the Gnostic Gospel of Thomas, "Break a stick and I am there." A monk once asked a Zen master, "What is Buddha?" He answered, "A stick of dried dung." The divine is everyplace where we open our eyes. You can think of it as emanating from God or nature; it doesn't matter, because there are no words or concepts that can contain it. The poet can only point to it with what exists between the words he or she writes. That contradiction is the beating of an angel's wings; it's the presence of the lover, the ecstasy of dogs running, the readiness of your name to release you. The poem is affirmation that there is more to reality than what we are taught to perceive or expect, that the impoverishment of our five senses can be enriched, and the very definition of ourselves can be amplified, and that we can increase our own significance by increasing the significance of the world.

Art in all of its forms has the ability to bring us back into focus, to open possibilities, provide ground to stand upon, and behold beingness, that most sacred of treasures. This is exactly what good poetry can accomplish. It can show you the aliveness of things, which we usually don't see, or see very superficially. Whether the poem is positive or negative is only secondary, what matters is that the poem is rendered with as much complete openness as possible. The poem doesn't have to be a "feel good" experience for it to have a spiritual dimension, for it to open the psyche to new realities. Pollyanna is not the patron saint of the arts. Poets needn't be moralists, or pillars of virtue, but rather instigators of new emotional patterns with which to approach the undeveloped faculties that lock us into time and culture. The cosmogenic push of the poem's instinct can see past the infantile ego of both the poet and the reader, if only momentarily, to show the potential that lies all around them. The poem is an ancient mediator in the long dispute between the cherished self and the deeper knowledge of the plentitude, which exists outside its narrow definition of reality.

We are taught to accept the view of the world we've inherited, the indicated circle of "reason" handed down generation after generation. For many, anything outside that protected boundary is unknown and therefore dangerous: "there be dragons" and a frenzy of likely horrors awaiting the traveller. Art has acted as both arbitrator and translator in that struggle with chaos, regardless of whether it's internal or external. At times, the more conservative among us are right, there are dragons out there. Sometimes the poem itself is a dragon, its green and regenerative fire burning away the petty notions we've accumulated about phenomenality. The motif of terra incognita is rich with possibilities, both positive and negative, but richer still is the chance for rebirth.

The poet must perform some degree of self-annihilation to experience the full fluidity of the poem rising out of the ground of being. The sanctum sanctorum cannot be reached with your name intact.

The poem as it is written down must precede you, not the other way around. If the poem doesn't lead the way, you're left with dross, with your opinions and beliefs formed during a lifetime of culturally acceptable ideas. To go your own way, you must be reborn to some degree each time you sit down to write a poem. Death and rebirth are a common theme in the traditions of all people. For the poet it is a necessary practice in order to cross over to the far-reaching space outside his or her personal views.

The sacred does not give itself readily to people whose heads are clogged with preconceptions and personal judgements on what a poem should be. Rather, the poet needs to be receptive to a long series of potential influences that can alter his or her basic percepts regarding what defines a poem. In part, the function and value of poetry is to cheat reason, to break away from its hold and censor. Reason is the serpent in the garden, it whispers in our ear that there is no larger panorama beyond its scope to behold. The pride of reason damages our ability to see the multi-dimensional possibilities inherent in our spirit. "Poetry heals the wounds inflicted by reason," to quote Novalis. To write, to really write, one must die to reason for a while in order to give birth to the ambiguous self, ready to explore all the unreasonable possibilities. The mystery lies in those redemptive words that come forth when we break free of our prejudices, allowing language to sharpen our sensibilities to a point of entry beyond mere reason.

Bounded by certain aspects of our daily consciousness, we become numb to much of the world; so much of it becomes dull and gives back no light. Art and poetry are not a panacea for all our ills, but they can help us to focus in on what's important, what calls to us around every corner, under every stone. Deepening our lives essentially means to be aware, to answer the call from life itself, to practise the veneration of its numerous forms. This has nothing to do with religion, per se; rather, religion and art grow out of this veneration, this deep need to bow our heads before wonder and being. Without art or religion, human beings still have this irresistible urge to acknowledge the awe they feel in the presence of creation.

An atheist can feel that as deeply as a believer, the magnitude of the experience can be exactly the same in either case. No amount of negation can push aside this longing for reverence, it wells up, regardless, in every human being. This yearning for the sacred is the driving force behind all true art, even if it isn't recognized as such. If we listen quietly we can hear that sigh of creation, world sustaining, spinning galaxies, balancing itself on the tip of a rabbit's hair, drifting to the ground on a birch leaf. The whole round of existence and every piece of it is revelation; every square inch is the totality of time and space nestled into form. Every atom is the ultimate expression of mystery, the mystery that things exist, that we have the ability to be conscious of them. The universe unfolds like the meaning of a single poem and that meaning is simply *to be*. The greatest mystery, held in every grain of cosmic dust, in every blade of grass, is existence itself. This is the first and last wonder, beyond words to describe; only the wordless poem can accomplish this. Only the poem we are always trying to write, but can only point to, that singularity immersed in the continuum of itself, without any possibility of secondary interpretations. Wordless, it comes to us without an attendant personality; without a meaning we can grasp with language. Yet we all know of it, feel it in times of intuition beyond the nature of names and forms, it is the connective tissue between heart and mind, stone and star. It is this living moment, alive now in the presence of all beings, in the *isness* of all objects.

NOTES

Don Domanski (1950–2020) was born and raised in Sydney, on Cape Breton Island, Nova Scotia, Canada. He lived briefly in Toronto, Vancouver and Wolfville, before settling in Halifax, Nova Scotia, where he lived for most of his life. Author of nine collections of poetry published during his lifetime, his work is infused with a deep and abiding interest in mythology, religion and esoteric philosophy, and has been translated into Arabic, Chinese, Czech, French, Portuguese and Spanish. He mentored other poets through the Banff Centre for the Arts Wired Writing Studio and the Writers' Federation of Nova Scotia Mentorship program.

Also a visual artist, his work often appeared on the covers of his books. He collected fossils for many years, before turning his attention to meteorites and Stone Age tools. He is credited with discovering the neural arch of a 350-million-year-old (Lower Carboniferous) amphibian previously thought to have gone extinct in the Devonian period.

His poetry collections *Wolf-Ladder* (1991) and *Stations of the Left Hand* (1994) were shortlisted for the Governor General's Award for Poetry, and in 1999 he received the Canadian Literary Award for Poetry from the Canadian Broadcasting Corporation. *All Our Wonder Unavenged* (2007) was honoured with the Governor General's Award, the Lieutenant Governor of Nova Scotia Masterworks Award, and the Atlantic Poetry Prize, and *Bite Down Little Whisper* (2013) won the J.M. Abraham Poetry Award.

SUNRISE AT SEA LEVEL: *Molpe.* In Greek mythology, one of the
three 'original' Sirens, as named by Apollonius (after Hesiod).

WALKING DOWN TO ACHERON: *I flow with grief.* Acheron, from the
Greek αχος ρεω, 'I flow with grief'.

ALL OUR WONDER UNAVENGED: *Proteus.* In Greek mythology, a
prophetic divinity. He could change himself into any shape he
chose, but if he were seized and held, he would assume his usual
form of an old man and foretell the future.

IN THE DREAM OF THE YELLOW BIRCHES: *Poems of the Late T'ang.* A
collection of Chinese poetry from the eighth and ninth centu-
ries A.D., translated by A.C. Graham.
The image of the imageless   unceasingly it continues. From the *Tao
Te Ching*, Chapter 14.

URSA IMMACULATE: *Julii.* One of the oldest families of Ancient
Rome. Julius Caesar and Gaius Julius Caesar Augustus were
members of this family.

MAGNUM MYSTERIUM: *piquerism.* The sexual practice of perforating
the skin of another person.

BITE DOWN LITTLE WHISPER: *The land that is nowhere, that is our true home.* From Chang Po-tuan, Chinese alchemist of the eleventh century.

FIELD NOTES: First published in the pamphlet, *Field Notes*, 2014, and subsequently in *Reliquiae* Volume 3, 2015.

BESTIARY OF THE RAINDROP: First published in *Reliquiae* Volume 4, 2016.

BIRTHDAY: First published in the pamphlet, *Nature and the Sacred*, 2017, and subsequently in *Reliquiae* Volume 8 Number 2, 2020.

A THIN PLACE: First published in *Reliquiae* Volume 5, 2017.

NOCTURNE: First published in *Reliquiae* Volume 6, 2018. *Doggerland.* An area of land, now submerged beneath the North Sea, that connected Great Britain to continental Europe. It was flooded by rising sea levels around 6500–6200 BCE.

THE GONENESS OF LOST THINGS: First published in *Reliquiae* Volume 6, 2018.

A PRAYER OF THANKS: First published in the *Selected Poems*, 2021. A gift from the poet to the editors on the Summer Solstice of 2017.

INDEX OF FIRST LINES